LEGAL ETHICS FOR THE REAL WORLD

BUILDING SKILLS THROUGH CASE STUDY

RENEE NEWMAN KNAKE
Joanne & Larry Doherty Chair in Legal Ethics
Professor of Law
Director, Outcomes and Assessments
University of Houston Law Center

M. ELLEN MURPHY
Assistant Dean of Instructional Technologies & Design
Wake Forest University School of Law

FOUNDATION
PRESS

© 2018 LEG, Inc. d/b/a West Academic
    444 Cedar Street, Suite 700
    St. Paul, MN 55101
    1-877-888-1330

Printed in the United States of America

ISBN: 978-1-64020-891-9

This book is dedicated to:

Grace and James
R.N.K.

Professor Joel Newman
M.E.M.

ACKNOWLEDGMENTS

We are incredibly grateful for Russ Pearce—without his generosity and belief in each of us individually this collaboration never would have occurred. Special thanks are also due to the following individuals for their support of this project: Staci Herr, Laura Holle, and Whitney Esson at Foundation Press, the Honorable Michelle Slaughter, Bruce Green, Mark Rabil, Kate Mewhinney, and Tessa Boury. We appreciate permissions to reprint materials that appear in the chapter appendices granted by the Public Information Office of the Florida Supreme Court, the Office of Public Information of the Supreme Court of Ohio, the Honorable Michelle Slaughter, and the Wake Forest University School of Law Elder Law Clinic. Thanks also to our respective law schools, the University of Houston Law Center and Wake Forest University School of Law, both for supporting this project and for their broad support of innovations in teaching and scholarship. Finally, we are grateful to our students for their feedback on portions of this project and their enthusiasm for experiential learning.

RENEE NEWMAN KNAKE
M. ELLEN MURPHY

INTRODUCTION

Hello, and welcome to this book of case studies based upon **real legal ethics**—stories about **lawyers and judges** from the **real** world. We believe legal ethics is the most important law school subject, and we are excited to guide your introduction to real-world lawyering through this topic.

Our Goals

Like other books in the Foundation Press "**Real World**" series, our goals here are simple.

We want to help you deepen your understanding of legal ethics, gain early literacy in basic lawyering skills, and develop a passion for real-world practice. This book contains seven case studies, each addressing some of the most pressing issues in modern legal ethics. Each case study combines critical thinking with practical skills based on recent, real-world ethical dilemmas, including advance conflicts waivers, advertising with new media, client confidentiality, lawyer substance abuse and wellbeing, social media use, prosecutorial discretion, and wrongful convictions.

Each case study also will provide opportunities to develop and practice "Early Lawyering Literacy" skills:

1. **Client Counseling**, including understanding the client's interests and how those interests exist within a broader, extra-legal context; communicating courses of action for a client to choose from that reflect those interests and goals; developing a plan to counsel the client; and anticipating a client's questions.

2. **Factual Investigation**, including identifying what facts are relevant and need to be identified, probing for concrete and detailed information from a client or third party, developing strategies for gathering the relevant facts, and understanding how factual investigation can shape the case theory.

3. **Legal Problem Solving**, including identifying the client's goals, diagnosing the core issues in a case, differentiating between legal and non-legal issues, foreseeing risks and contingencies, drawing from research and facts of the case to generate cogent strategies and courses of action (including non-legal alternatives when appropriate), and thinking creatively about the scope of potential solutions.

4. **Legal Reasoning**, including formulating and evaluating legal theories as applied to a specific set of facts, anticipating countervailing arguments, understanding the relationship among different sources of laws, and synthesizing legal arguments.

5. **Oral and Written Communication**, including speaking and writing to convey information clearly, concisely, and

persuasively with the audience in mind and in a range of contexts.

6. **Policymaking and Legal Reform**, including understanding how clients are impacted and respond to particular laws, understanding the likely intentions behind a particular statute, analyzing whether a client presents a situation that policymakers had not fully considered, and brainstorming potential statutory changes that would benefit the client.

7. **Reflective Practice**, including identifying personal strengths and weakness and areas for further development, and gaining insights into practice areas that bring satisfaction versus frustration.

8. **Research**, including basic online research, locating appropriate legal authority, and understanding differences between types of legal authority.

9. **Reviewing and Analyzing Legal Documents**, including developing proficiency in accessing and critically analyzing a range of different types of legal documents related to specific cases.

10. **Statutory Analysis**, including analyzing and interpreting statutes in a specific context, listing statutory elements for a particular cause of action to be viable, and identifying facts supporting and undercutting each element.

We believe that cultivating these skills with our case studies now as a law student will allow you to more easily develop them when you begin to practice law.

Most important, we hope the knowledge and skills acquired from this book serve as an important building block in your foundation for a rewarding and meaningful career in the law. Also, we want you to have fun learning more about the incredible profession you have chosen to join. Our students over the years have told us that the case studies and exercises we have included in this book are among the most informative, engaging, and fun—yes fun!—they have encountered during law school. We hope you agree.

How to Use This Book

We offer several suggestions for how to use this book. First, each chapter contains a wholly-independent case study, which can easily be used to supplement an upper level professional responsibility or legal ethics course. Second, book could be adopted on its own to teach an upper level seminar-style course with an experiential focus. Third, faculty wishing to incorporate an ethics-based experiential component into another course subject may select a single chapter for use. Each case study focuses on different early lawyering skills and substantive areas of legal ethics. Often, the studies are supplemented with actual legal documents including pleadings, opinions, rules, and other legal materials.

Similar to other books in the "Real World" series, as you work through case studies, you will see that some assignments ask you to try to find documents or perform other specific tasks on your own. If you get stuck, you can rely on one or more hints we provide or refer to the documents in the appendices in each chapter. We include them so that you can always make use of this book. But we want you to *try really hard* to find the information on your own, without relying on the hints and appendices. Developing the confidence and initiative to perform these tasks on your own efficiently is at the heart of excellent lawyering. (Also, to get you thinking and acting locally, we have included "Your Hometown" text boxes that you can use to apply different state laws.)

Please share your experiences with us. We welcome your thoughts and feedback—Renee Newman Knake <rknake@uh.edu> or Ellen Murphy <murphyme@wfu.edu>.

TABLE OF CONTENTS

ACKNOWLEDGMENTS V

INTRODUCTION VII

Chapter 1. Finding a Lawyer, Finding a Client 1
Background 1
The Case Study 4
    Part One: Where Do I Go to Find a Competent Lawyer? 4
    Part Two: Lawyer Advertising/Solicitation 6
    Part Three: Lawyer Referral Services 7
    Part Four: Creating a Professional Online Presence 8
    Documents Used in the Case Study 8
Appendix A. Ohio Rules of Professional Conduct 9
Appendix B. Ohio Ethics Opinion 31

Chapter 2. Ethics in Elder Law Representation 41
Background 41
The Case Study 42
    Part One: The Phone Call 43
    Part Two: The Client Intake 43
    Part Three: The Engagement Letter 46
    Part Four: A Slight Change of Facts 46
    Documents Used in the Case Study 47
Appendix A. Form Engagement Letter 49
Appendix B. *What If You Become Mentally Unable to Manage Your
    Affairs?* Client Handout 51

Chapter 3. Keeping Confidences: At What Cost? 53
Background 53
The Case Study 56
    Part One: What Do the Rules of Professional Conduct Provide? 56
    Part Two: Revisions to the New York Rule 58
    Part Three: What About the Attorney-Client Privilege? 60
    Part Four: An Alternative Approach 61
    Documents Used in the Case Study 61
Appendix A. Form Release of Attorney-Client Privilege 63

Chapter 4. Waiving a Conflict of Interest Before It Arises 65
Background 65
The Case Study 67
    Part One: Is the Advance Waiver Valid? 68
    Part Two: If Not, What Are the Consequences? 70
    Part Three: How to Avoid Disqualification in the Future 71
    Documents Used in the Case Study 72
Appendix A. *Sheppard, Mullin, Richter & Hampton, LLP v. J-M
    Manufacturing Co.*, 198 Cal.Rptr.3d 253 (2016) 73

Chapter 5. A Prosecutor's Fall from Grace 81
Background 81
The Case Study 82
    Part One: Are There Rules on Point? 83
    Part Two: The Duke Lacrosse Case 84
    Part Three: A Media Policy for Your Office 85
    Part Four: Electing Prosecutors 85

Chapter 6. The Facebooking Judge 87
Background 87
The Case Study 89
    Part One: The Judicial Discipline System 90
    Part Two: Judicial Conduct Codes and Advisory Opinions 91
    Part Three: Judicial Elections 92
    Part Four: The Appeal 93
    Part Five: Reform 93
    Documents Used in the Case Study 94
Appendix A. Texas State Commission on Judicial Conduct, Public
    Admonition and Order of Additional Education 95

Chapter 7. Substance Abuse and Lawyer Discipline 101
Background 101
The Case Study 102
    Part One: Bar Complaint 103
    Part Two: Role Play—Bar Grievance Committee Hearing 104
    Part Three: Appeal 104
    Part Four: Lawyers Assistance Programs 105
    Documents Used in the Case Study 105
Appendix A. Florida Bar Complaint 107

LEGAL ETHICS FOR THE REAL WORLD

BUILDING SKILLS THROUGH CASE STUDY

CHAPTER 1

FINDING A LAWYER, FINDING A CLIENT

ISSUE AREAS:

Access to Justice, Advertising, Attorney-Client Privilege, Confidentiality, Lawyer Referral Services, Solicitation, Websites

LEARNING OBJECTIVES:

1. Analyze professional conduct rules with an eye toward solving a particular problem not envisioned by rule drafters.

2. Apply the rules governing lawyer advertising/solicitation and lawyer referral in the context of online and electronic communication.

3. Develop your own online presence as a legal professional.

4. Draft effective disclosures for prospective clients' use of website features such as electronic submissions and live-chat forums.

5. Evaluate the implications of online communication between prospective clients and lawyers, including exposure to issues of attorney-client privilege and confidentiality.

6. Identify first amendment issues related to lawyer advertising and solicitation.

7. Recognize how clients find lawyers, and how lawyers find clients.

BACKGROUND

This case study will help you better understand how clients find lawyers, and how lawyers find clients, in an increasingly technology driven, Internet-based world. It will also expose you to issues such as client confidentiality and attorney-client privilege as well as rules on advertising and solicitation.

When individuals seek a lawyer, the main resource is an Internet search, even over asking for recommendations from family and friends, according to recent studies. Websites and blogs are important tools for lawyers to advertise their services.

While advertising is commonplace today, for much of the 20th century it was banned. When the American Bar Association adopted its Canons of Professional Responsibility in 1908, the canons included a prohibition on lawyer advertising and solicitation. Lawyers could communicate with family, friends, or existing clients about their services, and list a phone number in a directory, but nothing more.

The nationwide ban lasted until 1977, when the United States Supreme Court, in *Bates v. Arizona State Bar,* struck down the State Bar of Arizona's prohibition on lawyer advertising because it violated the first amendment.[1] There, two newly licensed attorneys sought to place a simple ad listing routine legal services and costs in the newspaper. This is a reproduction of their ad:

---

[1]   433 U.S. 350 (1977).

The Arizona State Bar argued that the advertisement was unprofessional and misleading. (Imagine what they would think of the billboards and late-night television commercials for lawyers that proliferate today!) The Supreme Court disagreed and, instead, found that permitting such advertising could help address a long-standing need for legal services by the middle class.

As it turns out, that same need for legal services endures nearly a half-century after *Bates* was decided. As many as 80% of American households continue to face two to three legal problems at any given time without assistance from a lawyer.[2] Lack of information is the primary reason, followed by cost.

One might be tempted to think that the Supreme Court was wrong to believe that advertising could expand access to legal services for the middle class since this need still endures. You should consider whether or not you believe that the Supreme Court got it wrong as you work through this case study.

A state-by-state patchwork of advertising restrictions currently exists in the United States, with no state banning lawyer advertising completely, but many placing significant restrictions on content and timing. At one end of the spectrum, some jurisdictions merely prohibit false or misleading advertising. At the other end, some jurisdictions impose heavy burdens, such as mandatory disclaimers, waiting periods, and pre-approval of advertising content by the regulatory authority.

The American Bar Association adopted Model Rules of Professional Conduct in 1983 to govern advertising and solicitation (see ABA Model Rules 7.1, 7.2 and 7.3). These rules permit advertising as long as it is not false or misleading. The ABA also has rules governing lawyer referral services and client confidentiality, which bear on how lawyers may advertise and solicit clients (see ABA Model Rules 1.5 and 1.6).

Advertising plays a significant role in the legal services markets. Lawyers spend millions of dollars annually on legal advertising, close to $800 million in 2016. While much of this goes to television commercials, increasingly lawyers invest in Internet advertising. (Indeed, legal terms dominate Google the keyword search terms purchases, with "nine out of the top 10 and 23 of the top 25" terms being legal terms in 2015. The most expensive phrase is "San Antonio car wreck attorney," which cost $670.)

As you engage with this exercise, feel free to depart from the specific instructions when conducting your research. Allow yourself to enjoy investigating, and follow your intuition. Take careful notes for your answers to the questions so that you can discuss your findings with your classmates and professor.

---

[2]   *See, e.g.*, Rebecca L. Sandefur, *Accessing Justice in the Contemporary USA: Findings from the Community Needs and Services Study*, SOCIAL SCIENCE RESEARCH NETWORK (2015), *available at* http://ssrn.com/abstract=2478040.

This case study will provide you with an opportunity to practice the following lawyering literacy skills: drafting electronic disclosures for legal websites research, legal problem solving, reviewing/analyzing legal documents, oral communication, policymaking and legal reform, statutory/rule analysis, reflective practice, and written communication.

THE CASE STUDY

You are a third year law student, and recently finished fall semester exams. While home in Ohio on winter break, you attend a party with friends from high school. One of your friends approaches you for advice. He was arrested for driving under the influence of alcohol, and has a hearing approaching in two weeks. He explains that he was not consuming alcohol at the time of the arrest, but that he had pulled an all-nighter and was drowsy, perhaps dozing off while behind the wheel. He doesn't know any lawyers personally, and asks if you would be willing to represent him. You explain that you can't represent anyone until you graduate from law school, pass the bar exam, and become licensed to practice. He then asks for your help in finding a lawyer who can represent him.

PART ONE: WHERE DO I GO TO FIND A COMPETENT LAWYER?

1. You now know that the main source for individuals seeking a lawyer is an Internet search. But where does one begin? Can you help your friend find a criminal defense lawyer by researching online? Write down the names of 3–4 attorneys you believe are competent to assist your friend. Only use the hints below if you get stuck.

> **HINT:** Begin by searching for criminal defense attorneys in Ohio in your preferred search browser such as Google Chrome, Firefox, or Safari. What results appear first in your search? Do you know why the results appear in this order? Can you make an informed, trustworthy recommendation for your friend based upon the information available online you've found through this initial search?

> **HINT:** Can you find a resource listing attorneys in Ohio that does not rely on Internet search rankings?
>
> If you get stuck, go to this site:
>
> https://www.ohiobar.org/ForPublic/Pages/ForPublic.aspx

> **YOUR HOMETOWN:** Conduct the same searches for a criminal defense attorney in your hometown. How are the results similar or different?

2. Just because a lawyer's website is appealing does not necessarily guarantee that the lawyer will provide competent services, or even that the lawyer holds an active law license. Before recommending a lawyer to your friend, at a minimum, you want to confirm that the lawyer is currently licensed to practice in Ohio and that the lawyer has not been disciplined. How can you determine this? If you find an attorney with a past disciplinary sanction but an active law license, consider whether you would recommend the attorney to your friend. Why or why not?

> **HINT:** Every jurisdiction in the United States maintains a list of attorneys licensed to practice in that jurisdiction, most of which can be found online. Typically this is maintained by a state bar association or a state licensing authority. Use the list of 3–4 attorneys from your initial search in Part One, and determine whether they hold an active law license in Ohio with no disciplinary sanctions.
>
> If you get stuck, go to this site:
>
> https://www.supremecourt.ohio.gov/AttySvcs/AttyReg/

> **YOUR HOMETOWN:** Does your jurisdiction maintain an online database of lawyers online? If not, choose a nearby jurisdiction. Locate the online database and explore how it differs from Ohio's attorney registration website. Is your hometown located in a state with a mandatory/integrated bar association? If so, then the state bar association is the licensing authority. If your hometown is in a state like Ohio with a voluntary bar association, the licensing authority will be a body designated by the highest state court. What is the difference between a mandatory/integrated bar association and a voluntary bar association?

3. Your friend asks you to find an attorney with a website where he can submit his information via an electronic contact form or through a live chat tool so that he does not have to take an afternoon off from work to visit the attorney's office. Do any of the attorneys on your list have these features on their websites? If not, continue searching until you find examples of both an electronic form and a live chat. Feel free to search for other attorneys in Ohio or your hometown to complete this step.

> **HINT:** Try interacting with both an electronic contact form and a live chat tool to see how they work; be sure to explain that you are not seeking legal services but are learning about how the processes work as part of a law school class assignment. Find out the following information, if you can: (1) whether you are communicating with a lawyer or an assistant (or perhaps even a third party who is not employed directly by the lawyer); (2) whether any disclosure

appears regarding attorney/client privilege or confidentiality, either before or after you submit the form; and (3) whether there is any limit on the number of characters allowed into the submission field. Why might this information be important to a prospective client? Do you have any concerns about the possible formation of a lawyer-client relationship or disclosure of confidential information?

LEARN MORE: For a different sort of online communication to obtain legal help, visit Do Not Pay: http://www.donotpay.com/. Enter basic information to receive help on your friend's behalf. First, click on "learn more." Note the response you receive. What concerns do you have? Second, try requesting help with a parking ticket and again click on "learn more." What happens differently this time? You will be prompted to provide a location, date, and name—enter your hometown, today's date, and a pseudonym. Print out the appeal letter that is prepared. Who prepared this letter? What is a "bot"? What concerns do you have about this letter?

PART TWO: LAWYER ADVERTISING/SOLICITATION

1.   Your friend mentions that the day after his arrest he received a text message from an attorney offering to represent him. He asks you whether he should just use this attorney, since the attorney must be somewhat familiar already with his case given that he was able to locate his cell phone number. What do you suggest to your friend? Are lawyers permitted to contact prospective clients in this way?

HINT: The ABA Model Rules, while not binding, are models that most jurisdictions base their rules upon, and it can be helpful to look at them for guidance. (The ABA Model Rules are also tested on the Multi-State Professional Responsibility Exam, which is another reason for you to be familiar with them!) You can find the most up-to-date versions on the ABA website here:

https://www.americanbar.org/groups/professional_responsibility/ publications/model_rules_of_professional_conduct/model_rules_of_ professional_conduct_table_of_contents.html

Look at Model Rules 7.1, 7.2, and 7.3 to see if you can determine whether or not an attorney can text a prospective client.

HINT: Each state and Washington DC has adopted its own unique set of professional conduct rules, even though most are based upon the ABA Model Rules. The corresponding Ohio advertising and solicitation rules are included in Appendix A of this case study. Compare how they are the same or different than the ABA Model Rules.

HINT: Often professional conduct rules do not keep up with the fast pace of technology advances. The process for amending a professional conduct rule can take several years of study, drafting, and debates before a change is made. Sometimes the state ethics authority will issue an opinion to provide guidance for lawyers when it is unclear how to apply an older rule to new technology. An opinion on Direct Contact with Prospective Clients in Text Messages issued by the Supreme Court of Ohio Board of Commissioners on Grievances and Discipline is reproduced in Appendix B.

YOUR HOMETOWN: Conduct the same search for the advertising and solicitation rules that apply in your hometown. How are the rules similar or different?

PART THREE: LAWYER REFERRAL SERVICES

1. One of the top results from your search in Part One likely appeared from a website called http://Avvo.com. Search the Avvo website for the same list of 3–4 attorneys you searched for on the Ohio attorney registration website. Even if you do not use a service like Avvo, it should cause you to think about how you and your colleagues portray yourselves to the public, and prospective clients, both online and off line. What information on the Avvo site is helpful to recommending a lawyer for your friend? How is this different from what you found on their personal websites? Can you now make an informed, trustworthy recommendation based upon the information you've located?

HINT: What sort of entity is Avvo? Who controls Avvo? Where does the information available on Avvo come from? How many lawyers are profiled on Avvo? See what information you can find directly on the Avvo.com site.

HINT: Does Avvo's lawyer referral service comply with Ohio lawyer ethics rules?

If you get stuck, go to this site:

http://www.supremecourt.ohio.gov/Boards/BOC/Advisory_Opinions/2016/Op_16-003.pdf

HINT: State ethics regulators sometimes disagree about how existing rules should be applied to technology advances. For example, as Facebook grew in popularity, lawyers and judges began using it even before a state regulator had opined on its efficacy. The

Florida Supreme Court Judicial Ethics Advisory Committee was among the first to do so in 2009, initially opining that judges should not 'friend' lawyers on Facebook. Subsequent opinions from other states were less restrictive, urging lawyers and judges to use caution when using social media but not prohibiting it. Can you find opinions from other jurisdictions about Avvo's compliance with ethics rules? Identify one jurisdiction and explain how it views Avvo's compliance.

If you get stuck, go to these sites:

https://efactssc-public.flcourts.org/casedocuments/2016/1470/2016-1470_response_47140.pdf

http://www.floridasupremecourt.org/decisions/2015/sc14-2126.pdf

PART FOUR: CREATING A PROFESSIONAL ONLINE PRESENCE

1.   After helping your friend navigate the Internet to find potential attorneys, you begin to think about your own online presence. Reflect upon how you already appear online by looking up your name in the same Internet search tool that you used in Part One. Also consider social media sites that are not kept private, such as Facebook, Twitter, Instagram, LinkedIn, and others. Not only will prospective clients search for you online; so will potential employers. Now is the time to make sure your online presence reflects the professional you are becoming during your time in law school. Consider setting up a Google Alert for your name: https://www.google.com/alerts.

2.   While on winter break, you are working part time for a local attorney. She mentions that she wants to make her website more interactive for prospective clients, but isn't sure how best to do so and notes that neither the ABA nor Ohio have specific rules designed especially for website marketing. You describe to her what you have learned from your experience helping your friend find a criminal defense lawyer. She asks you assist with adding an electronic submission form and a live chat feature. She wants to make sure that these tools are engaging and user-friendly for prospective clients as well as compliant with any existing ethics rules. Draft a brief 2–3 paragraph memo to her recommending best practices for using these tools on her website, including proposed language for any disclosures or disclaimers you believe are necessary.

DOCUMENTS USED IN THE CASE STUDY

Appendix A: Ohio Rules 1.6, 7.1, 7.2. 7.3

Appendix B: Ohio Ethics Opinion

APPENDIX A

OHIO RULES OF PROFESSIONAL CONDUCT

OHIO RULES OF PROFESSIONAL CONDUCT

(Effective February 1, 2007; as amended effective May 2, 2017)

TABLE OF CONTENTS

	Preamble: A Lawyer's Responsibilities; Scope	1
1.0	Terminology	5

Client-Lawyer Relationship

1.1	Competence	11
1.2	Scope of Representation and Allocation of Authority Between Client and Lawyer	14
1.3	Diligence	18
1.4	Communication	20
1.5	Fees and Expenses	24
1.6	Confidentiality of Information	31
1.7	Conflict of Interest: Current Clients	39
1.8	Conflict of Interest: Current Clients: Specific Rules	50
1.9	Duties to Former Clients	61
1.10	Imputation of Conflicts of Interest: General Rule	65
1.11	Special Conflicts of Interest for Former and Current Government Officers and Employees	70
1.12	Former Judge, Arbitrator, Mediator, or Other Third-Party Neutral	74
1.13	Organization as Client	77
1.14	Client with Diminished Capacity	82
1.15	Safekeeping Funds and Property	86
1.16	Declining or Terminating Representation	92
1.17	Sale of Law Practice	96
1.18	Duties to Prospective Client	102

Counselor

2.1	Advisor	105
2.2	[Reserved for future use; no corresponding ABA Model Rule]	
2.3	Evaluation for Use by Third Persons	107
2.4	Lawyer Serving as Arbitrator, Mediator, or Third-Party Neutral	110

Advocate

3.1	Meritorious Claims and Contentions	112
3.2	Expediting Litigation [Not Adopted; See Note]	113
3.3	Candor toward the Tribunal	114
3.4	Fairness to Opposing Party and Counsel	119
3.5	Impartiality and Decorum of the Tribunal	121
3.6	Trial Publicity	124

Comment

[1] This rule governs the disclosure by a lawyer of information relating to the representation of a client during the lawyer's representation of the client. See Rule 1.18 for the lawyer's duties with respect to information provided to the lawyer by a prospective client, Rule 1.9(c)(2) for the lawyer's duty not to reveal information relating to the lawyer's prior representation of a former client, and Rules 1.8(b) and 1.9(c)(1) for the lawyer's duties with respect to the use of such information to the disadvantage of clients and former clients.

[2] A fundamental principle in the client-lawyer relationship is that, in the absence of the client's informed consent, the lawyer must not reveal information relating to the representation. See Rule 1.0(f) for the definition of informed consent. This contributes to the trust that is the hallmark of the client-lawyer relationship. The client is thereby encouraged to seek legal assistance and to communicate fully and frankly with the lawyer even as to embarrassing or legally damaging subject matter. The lawyer needs this information to represent the client effectively and, if necessary, to advise the client to refrain from wrongful conduct. Almost without exception, clients come to lawyers in order to determine their rights and what is, in the complex of laws and regulations, deemed to be legal and correct.

[3] The principle of client-lawyer confidentiality is given effect by related bodies of law: the attorney-client privilege, the work-product doctrine, and the rule of confidentiality established in professional ethics. The attorney-client privilege and work-product doctrine apply in judicial and other proceedings in which a lawyer may be called as a witness or otherwise required to produce evidence concerning a client. The rule of client-lawyer confidentiality applies in situations other than those where evidence is sought from the lawyer through compulsion of law. The confidentiality rule, for example, applies not only to matters communicated in confidence by the client but also to all information relating to the representation, whatever its source. A lawyer may not disclose such information except as authorized or required by the Ohio Rules of Professional Conduct or other law. See also Scope.

[4] Division (a) prohibits a lawyer from revealing information relating to the representation of a client. This prohibition also applies to disclosures by a lawyer that do not in themselves reveal protected information but could reasonably lead to the discovery of such information by a third person. A lawyer's use of a hypothetical to discuss issues relating to the representation is permissible so long as there is no reasonable likelihood that the listener will be able to ascertain the identity of the client or the situation involved.

Authorized Disclosure

[5] Except to the extent that the client's instructions or special circumstances limit that authority, a lawyer is impliedly authorized to make disclosures about a client when appropriate in carrying out the representation. In some situations, for example, a lawyer may be impliedly authorized to admit a fact that cannot properly be disputed or to make a disclosure that facilitates a satisfactory conclusion to a matter. Lawyers in a firm may, in the course of the firm's practice, disclose to each other information relating to a client of the firm, unless the client has instructed that particular information be confined to specified lawyers.

Disclosure Adverse to Client

[6]   Permitting lawyers to reveal information relating to the representation of clients may create a chilling effect on the client-lawyer relationship, and discourage clients from revealing confidential information to their lawyers at a time when the clients should be making a full disclosure. Although the public interest is usually best served by a strict rule requiring lawyers to preserve the confidentiality of information relating to the representation of their clients, the confidentiality rule is subject to limited exceptions. Division (b)(1) recognizes the overriding value of life and physical integrity and permits disclosure reasonably necessary to prevent reasonably certain death or substantial bodily harm. Such harm is reasonably certain to occur if it will be suffered imminently or if there is a present and substantial threat that a person will suffer such harm at a later date if the lawyer fails to take action necessary to eliminate the threat. Thus, a lawyer who knows that a client has discharged toxic waste into a town's water supply may reveal this information to the authorities if there is a present and substantial risk that a person who drinks the water will contract a life-threatening or debilitating disease and the lawyer's disclosure is necessary to eliminate the threat or reduce the number of victims.

[7]   Division (b)(2) recognizes the traditional "future crime" exception, which permits lawyers to reveal the information necessary to prevent the commission of the crime by a client or a third party.

[8]   Division (b)(3) addresses the situation in which the lawyer does not learn of the illegal or fraudulent act of a client until after the client has used the lawyer's services to further it. Although the client no longer has the option of preventing disclosure by refraining from the wrongful conduct [see Rule 4.1], there will be situations in which the loss suffered by the affected person can be mitigated. In such situations, the lawyer may disclose information relating to the representation to the extent necessary to enable the affected persons to mitigate or recoup their losses. Division (b)(3) does not apply when a person is accused of or has committed an illegal or fraudulent act and thereafter employs a lawyer for representation concerning that conduct. In addition, division (b)(3) does not apply to a lawyer who has been engaged by an organizational client to investigate an alleged violation of law by the client or a constituent of the client.

[9]   A lawyer's confidentiality obligations do not preclude a lawyer from securing confidential legal advice about the lawyer's personal responsibility to comply with these rules. In most situations, disclosing information to secure such advice will be impliedly authorized for the lawyer to carry out the representation. Even when the disclosure is not impliedly authorized, division (b)(4) permits such disclosure because of the importance of a lawyer's compliance with the Ohio Rules of Professional Conduct.

[10]   Where a legal claim or disciplinary charge alleges complicity of the lawyer in the conduct of a client or a former client or other misconduct of the lawyer involving representation of the client or a former client, the lawyer may respond to the extent the lawyer reasonably believes necessary to establish a defense. Such a charge can arise in a civil, criminal, disciplinary, or other proceeding and can be based on a wrong allegedly committed by the lawyer against the client or on a wrong alleged by a third person, for example, a person claiming to have

been defrauded by the lawyer and client acting together. The lawyer's right to respond arises when an assertion of such complicity has been made. Division (b)(5) does not require the lawyer to await the commencement of an action or proceeding that charges such complicity, so that the defense may be established by responding directly to a third party who has made such an assertion. The right to defend also applies, of course, where a proceeding has been commenced.

[11]   A lawyer entitled to a fee is permitted by division (b)(5) to prove the services rendered in an action to collect it. This aspect of the rule expresses the principle that the beneficiary of a fiduciary relationship may not exploit it to the detriment of the fiduciary.

[12]   Other law may require that a lawyer disclose information about a client. Whether such a law supersedes Rule 1.6 is a question of law beyond the scope of these rules. When disclosure of information relating to the representation appears to be required by other law, the lawyer must discuss the matter with the client to the extent required by Rule 1.4. If, however, the other law supersedes this rule and requires disclosure, division (b)(6) permits the lawyer to make such disclosures as are necessary to comply with the law.

Detection of Conflicts of Interest

[13]   Division (b)(7) recognizes that lawyers in different firms may need to disclose limited information to each other to detect and resolve conflicts of interest, such as when a lawyer is considering an association with another firm, two or more firms are considering a merger, or a lawyer is considering the purchase of a law practice. See Rule 1.17, Comment [7]. Under these circumstances, lawyers and law firms are permitted to disclose limited information, but only once substantive discussions regarding the new relationship have occurred. Any such disclosure should ordinarily include no more than the identity of the persons and entities involved in a matter, a brief summary of the general issues involved, and information about whether the matter has terminated. Even this limited information should be disclosed only to the extent reasonably necessary to detect and resolve conflicts of interest that might arise from the possible new relationship. Moreover, the disclosure of any information is prohibited if it would compromise the attorney-client privilege or otherwise prejudice the client (*e.g.*, the fact that a corporate client is seeking advice on a corporate takeover that has not been publicly announced; that a person has consulted a lawyer about the possibility of a divorce before the person's intentions are known to the person's spouse; or that a person has consulted a lawyer about a criminal investigation that has not led to a public charge). Under those circumstances, division (a) prohibits disclosure unless the client or former client gives informed consent. A lawyer's fiduciary duty to the lawyer's firm may also govern a lawyer's conduct when exploring an association with another firm and is beyond the scope of these rules.

[14]   Any information disclosed pursuant to division (b)(7) may be used or further disclosed only to the extent necessary to detect and resolve conflicts of interest. Division (b)(7) does not restrict the use of information acquired by means independent of any disclosure pursuant to division (b)(7). Division (b)(7) also does not affect the disclosure of information within a law firm when the disclosure is otherwise authorized, such as when a lawyer in a firm discloses information to another lawyer in the same firm to detect and resolve conflicts of interest that could arise in connection with undertaking a new representation. See Comment [5].

[15]   A lawyer may be ordered to reveal information relating to the representation of a client by a court or by another tribunal or governmental entity claiming authority pursuant to other law to compel the disclosure. Absent informed consent of the client to do otherwise, the lawyer should assert on behalf of the client all nonfrivolous claims that the order is not authorized by other law or that the information sought is protected against disclosure by the attorney-client privilege or other applicable law. In the event of an adverse ruling, the lawyer must consult with the client about the possibility of appeal to the extent required by Rule 1.4. Unless review is sought, however, division (b)(6) permits the lawyer to comply with the court's order.

[16]   Division (b) permits disclosure only to the extent the lawyer reasonably believes the disclosure is necessary to accomplish one of the purposes specified. Where practicable, the lawyer should first seek to persuade the client to take suitable action to obviate the need for disclosure. A disclosure adverse to the client's interest should be no greater than the lawyer reasonably believes necessary to accomplish the purpose. If the disclosure will be made in connection with a judicial proceeding, the disclosure should be made in a manner that limits access to the information to the tribunal or other persons having a need to know it and appropriate protective orders or other arrangements should be sought by the lawyer to the fullest extent practicable. Before making a disclosure under division (b)(1), (2), or (3), a lawyer for an organization should ordinarily bring the issue of taking suitable action to higher authority within the organization, including, if warranted by the circumstances, to the highest authority that can act on behalf of the organization as determined by applicable law.

[17]   Division (b) permits but does not require the disclosure of information relating to a client's representation to accomplish the purposes specified in divisions (b)(1) through (b)(6). In exercising the discretion conferred by this rule, the lawyer may consider such factors as the nature of the lawyer's relationship with the client and with those who might be injured by the client, the lawyer's own involvement in the transaction, and factors that may extenuate the conduct in question. A lawyer's decision not to disclose as permitted by division (b) does not violate this rule. Disclosure may be required, however, by other rules. Some rules require disclosure only if such disclosure would be permitted by division (b). See Rules 4.1(b), 8.1 and 8.3. Rule 3.3, on the other hand, requires disclosure in some circumstances regardless of whether such disclosure is permitted by this rule.

Acting Competently to Preserve Confidentiality

[18]   Division (c) requires a lawyer to act competently to safeguard information relating to the representation of a client against unauthorized access by third parties and against inadvertent or unauthorized disclosure by the lawyer or other persons who are participating in the representation of the client or who are subject to the lawyer's supervision. See Rules 1.1, 5.1, and 5.3. The unauthorized access to or the inadvertent or unauthorized disclosure of information related to the representation of a client does not constitute a violation of division (c) if the lawyer has made reasonable efforts to prevent the access or disclosure. Factors to be considered in determining the reasonableness of the lawyer's efforts include, but are not limited to, the sensitivity of the information, the likelihood of disclosure if additional safeguards are not employed, the cost of employing additional safeguards, the difficulty of implementing the

safeguards, and the extent to which the safeguards adversely affect the lawyer's ability to represent clients (*e.g.*, by making a device or important piece of software excessively difficult to use). A client may require the lawyer to implement special security measures not required by this rule or may give informed consent to forego security measures that would otherwise be required by this rule. Whether a lawyer may be required to take additional steps to safeguard a client's information in order to comply with other law, such as state or federal laws that govern data privacy or that impose specific notification requirements upon the loss of or unauthorized access to electronic information is beyond the scope of these rules. For a lawyer's duties when sharing information with nonlawyers outside the lawyer's own firm see Rule 5.3, Comments [3] and [4].

[19]   When transmitting a communication that includes information relating to the representation of a client, the lawyer must take reasonable precautions to prevent the information from coming into the hands of unintended recipients. This duty, however, does not require that the lawyer use special security measures if the method of communication affords a reasonable expectation of privacy. Special circumstances, however, may warrant special precautions. Factors to be considered in determining the reasonableness of the lawyer's expectation of confidentiality include the sensitivity of the information and the extent to which the privacy of the communication is protected by law or by a confidentiality agreement. A client may require the lawyer to implement special security measures not required by this rule or may give informed consent to the use of a means of communication that would otherwise be prohibited by this rule. Whether a lawyer may be required to take additional steps in order to comply with other law, such as state and federal laws governing data privacy, is beyond the scope of these rules.

Former Client

[20]   The duty of confidentiality continues after the client-lawyer relationship has terminated. See Rule 1.9(c)(2). See Rule 1.9(c)(1) for the prohibition against using such information to the disadvantage of the former client.

Comparison to former Ohio Code of Professional Responsibility

Rule 1.6 replaces Canon 4 (A Lawyer Should Preserve the Confidences and Secrets of a Client), including DR 4-101 (Preservation of Confidences and Secrets of a Client) and ECs 4-1 to 4-6 of the Ohio Code of Professional Responsibility.

Rule 1.6(a) generally corresponds to DR 4-101(A) by protecting the confidences and secrets of a client under the rubric of "information relating to the representation." To clarify that this includes privileged information, the rule is amended to add the phrase, "including information protected by the attorney-client privilege under applicable law." Rule 1.6(a) also corresponds to DR 4-101(B) by prohibiting the lawyer from revealing such information. Use of client information is governed by Rule 1.8(b).

Rule 1.6(a) further corresponds to DR 4-101(C)(1) by exempting disclosures where the client gives "informed consent," including situations where disclosure is "impliedly authorized" by the client's informed consent.

Rule 1.6(b) addresses the exceptions to confidentiality and generally corresponds to DR 4-101(C)(2) to (4). Rule 1.6(b)(1) is new and has no comparable Code provision. Rule 1.6(b)(2) is the future crime exception and corresponds to DR 4-101(C)(3), with the addition of "or other person" from the Model Rule. Rule 1.6(b)(3) expands on the provisions of DR 7-102(B)(1) by permitting disclosure of information related to the representation of a client, including privileged information, to mitigate substantial injury to the financial interests or property of another that has been caused by the client's illegal or fraudulent act and the client has used the lawyer's services to further the commission of the illegal or fraudulent act.

Rule 1.6(b)(4) is new, and codifies the common practice of lawyers to consult with other lawyers about compliance with these rules. Rule 1.6(b)(5) tracks DR 4-101(C)(4), adding "any disciplinary matter" to clarify the rule's application in that situation. Rule 1.6(b)(6) is the same as DR 4-101(C)(2).

Rule 1.6(c) makes explicit that other rules create mandatory rather than discretionary disclosure duties. For example, Rules 3.3 and 4.1 correspond to DR 7-102(B), which requires disclosure of client fraud in certain circumstances.

Comparison to ABA Model Rules of Professional Conduct

The additions to Rule 1.6(a) are intended to clarify that "information relating to the representation" includes information protected by the attorney-client privilege.

The exceptions to confidentiality in Rule 1.6(b) generally track those found in the Model Rule, although two of Ohio's exceptions [Rules 1.6(b)(2) and (3)] permit more disclosure than the Model Rule allows.

Rule 1.6(b)(1) is the same as the Model Rule and reflects the policy that threatened death or serious bodily harm, regardless of criminality, create the occasion for a lawyer's discretionary disclosure. Nineteen jurisdictions have such a provision.

Rule 1.6(b)(2) differs from the Model Rule by maintaining the traditional formulation of the future crime exception currently found in DR 4-101(C)(3), rather than the future crime/fraud provision in Model Rule 1.6(b)(2) that is tied to "substantial injury to the financial interests of another." Twenty-two jurisdictions, including Ohio, opt for this stand-alone future crime exception. This exception is retained because it mirrors the public policy embodied in the criminal law.

Rule 1.6(b)(3) differs from Model Rule 1.6(b)(3) in two ways: it deletes the words "prevent" and "rectify;" and it allows for disclosure to mitigate the effects of the client's commission of an illegal (as opposed to criminal) or fraudulent act. The prevention of fraud is deleted from Rule 1.6(b)(3) because it is addressed in Rule 4.1(b). The extension of "criminal" to "illegal" is consistent with the use of the term "illegal" in Rules 1.2(d), 1.16(b), 4.1(b), and 8.4(b), but it is not found in either the Model Rule or Ohio disciplinary rules as an exception to confidentiality. Only two jurisdictions have included illegal conduct as justification for disclosure in Rule 1.6.

Rule 1.6(b)(4) is similar to the Model Rule.

Rule 1.6(b)(5) adds "disciplinary matter" to clarify the application of the exception.

Rule 1.6(c) is substantially the same as Model Rule 1.6(b)(6), except that it clarifies the mandatory disclosure required by other rules.

VII. INFORMATION ABOUT LEGAL SERVICES

RULE 7.1: COMMUNICATIONS CONCERNING A LAWYER'S SERVICES

A lawyer shall not make or use a false, misleading, or nonverifiable communication about the lawyer or the lawyer's services. A communication is false or misleading if it contains a material misrepresentation of fact or law or omits a fact necessary to make the statement considered as a whole not materially misleading.

Comment

[1]   This rule governs all communications about a lawyer's services, including advertising permitted by Rule 7.2. Whatever means are used to make known a lawyer's services, statements about them must be truthful.

[2]   Truthful statements that are misleading are also prohibited by this rule. A truthful statement is misleading if it omits a fact necessary to make the lawyer's communication considered as a whole not materially misleading. A truthful statement is also misleading if there is a substantial likelihood that it will lead a reasonable person to formulate a specific conclusion about the lawyer or the lawyer's services for which there is no reasonable factual foundation.

[3]   An advertisement that truthfully reports a lawyer's achievements on behalf of clients or former clients may be misleading if presented so as to lead a reasonable person to form an unjustified expectation that the same results could be obtained for other clients in similar matters without reference to the specific factual and legal circumstances of each client's case. Similarly, an unsubstantiated comparison of the lawyer's services or fees with the services or fees of other lawyers may be misleading if presented with such specificity as would lead a reasonable person to conclude that the comparison can be substantiated. The inclusion of an appropriate disclaimer or qualifying language may preclude a finding that a statement is likely to create unjustified expectations or otherwise mislead the public.

[4]   Characterization of rates or fees chargeable by the lawyer or law firm such as "cut-rate," "lowest," "giveaway," "below cost," "discount," or "special" is misleading.

[5]   See also Rule 8.4(e) for the prohibition against stating or implying an ability to influence improperly a government agency or official or to achieve results by means that violate the Ohio Rules of Professional Conduct or other law.

Comparison to former Ohio Code of Professional Responsibility

Rule 7.1 corresponds to DR 2-101. Rule 7.1 does not contain the prohibitions found in DR 2-101 on client testimonials or self-laudatory claims. However, the rule does retain the DR 2-101 prohibition on unverifiable claims.

In addition, Rule 7.1 contains none of the other directives found in DR 2-101(B), the definition of misleading found in DR 2-101(C) (see comment [2] of Rule 7.1), or the directives found in DR 2-101(D), (E), and (G).

For DR 2-101(F) and DR 2-101(H) see Rule 7.3.

Comparison to ABA Model Rules of Professional Conduct

Rule 7.1 is similar to Model Rule 7.1 except for the inclusion of a prohibition on the use of nonverifiable communications about the lawyer or the lawyer's services.

RULE 7.2: ADVERTISING AND RECOMMENDATION OF PROFESSIONAL EMPLOYMENT

(a)   Subject to the requirements of Rules 7.1 and 7.3, a lawyer may advertise services through *written*, recorded, or electronic communication, including public media.

(b)   A lawyer shall not give anything of value to a person for recommending the lawyer's services except that a lawyer may pay any of the following:

    (1)   the *reasonable* costs of advertisements or communications permitted by this rule;

    (2)   the usual charges of a legal service plan;

    (3)   the usual charges for a nonprofit or lawyer referral service that complies with Rule XVI of the Supreme Court Rules for the Government of the Bar of Ohio;

    (4)   for a law practice in accordance with Rule 1.17.

(c)   Any communication made pursuant to this rule shall include the name and office address of at least one lawyer or *law firm* responsible for its content.

(d)   A lawyer shall not seek employment in connection with a matter in which the lawyer or *law firm* does not intend to participate actively in the representation, but that the lawyer or *law firm* intends to refer to other counsel. This provision shall not apply to organizations listed in Rules 7.2(b)(2) or (3) or if the advertisement is in furtherance of a transaction permitted by Rule 1.17.

Comment

[1]   To assist the public in learning about and obtaining legal services, lawyers should be allowed to make known their services not only through reputation but also through organized information campaigns in the form of advertising. Advertising involves an active quest for clients, contrary to the tradition that a lawyer should not seek clientele. However, the public's need to know about legal services can be fulfilled in part through advertising. This need is particularly acute in the case of persons of moderate means who have not made extensive use of legal services. The interest in expanding public information about legal services ought to prevail over considerations of tradition. Nevertheless, advertising by lawyers entails the risk of practices that are misleading or overreaching.

[2]   This rule permits public dissemination of information concerning a lawyer's name or firm name, address, email address, website, and telephone number; the kinds of services the lawyer will undertake; the basis on which the lawyer's fees are determined, including prices for specific services and payment and credit arrangements; a lawyer's foreign language ability;

names of references and, with their consent, names of clients regularly represented; and other information that might invite the attention of those seeking legal assistance.

[3]   Questions of effectiveness and taste in advertising are matters of speculation and subjective judgment. Some jurisdictions have had extensive prohibitions against television and other forms of advertising, advertising going beyond specified facts about a lawyer, or "undignified" advertising. Television, the Internet, and other forms of electronic communication are among the most powerful media for getting information to the public, particularly persons of low and moderate income. Prohibiting television, Internet, or other forms of electronic advertising would impede the flow of information about legal services to many sectors of the public. Limiting the information that may be advertised has a similar effect and assumes that the bar can accurately forecast the kind of information that the public would regard as relevant. But see Rule 7.3(a) for the prohibition against solicitation through a real-time electronic exchange initiated by the lawyer.

[4]   Neither this rule nor Rule 7.3 prohibits communications authorized by law, such as notice to members of a class in class action litigation.

Paying Others to Recommend a Lawyer

[5]   Except as provided by these rules, lawyers are not permitted to give anything of value to another for recommending the lawyer's services or channeling professional work in a manner that violates Rule 7.3. A communication contains a recommendation if it endorses or vouches for a lawyer's credentials, abilities, competence, character, or other professional qualities. A reciprocal referral agreement between lawyers, or between a lawyer and a nonlawyer, is prohibited. *Cf.* Rule 1.5.

[5A]   Division (b)(1) allows a lawyer to pay for advertising and communications permitted by this rule, including the costs of print directory listings, on-line directory listings, newspaper ads, television and radio airtime, domain-name registrations, sponsorship fees, Internet-based advertisements, and group advertising. A lawyer may compensate employees, agents, and vendors who are engaged to provide marketing or client-development services, such as publicists, public-relations personnel, business-development staff and website designers. Moreover, a lawyer may pay others for generating client leads, including Internet-based client leads, provided the lead generator does not recommend the lawyer, any payment to the lead generator is consistent with Rules 1.5 and 5.4, and the lead generator's communications are consistent with Rule 7.1. To comply with Rule 7.1, a lawyer shall not pay a lead generator that states, implies, or creates a reasonable impression that it is recommending the lawyer, is making the referral without payment from the lawyer, or has analyzed a person's legal problems when determining which lawyer should receive the referral. See Rules 5.3 and 8.4(a).

[6]   A lawyer may pay the usual charges of a legal service plan or a nonprofit or qualified lawyer referral service. A legal service plan is a prepaid or group legal service plan or a similar delivery system that assists people who seek to secure legal representation. A lawyer referral service, on the other hand, is any organization that holds itself out to the public as a lawyer referral service. Such referral services are understood by the public to be consumer-oriented organizations that provide unbiased referrals to lawyers with appropriate experience in

the subject matter of the representation and afford other client protections, such as complaint procedures or malpractice insurance requirements. Consequently, this rule only permits a lawyer to pay the usual charges of a nonprofit or qualified lawyer referral service. A qualified lawyer referral service is one that is approved pursuant to Rule XVI of the Supreme Court Rules for the Government of the Bar of Ohio. Relative to fee sharing, see Rule 5.4(a)(5).

[7]   A lawyer who accepts assignments or referrals from a legal service plan or referrals from a lawyer referral service must act reasonably to assure that the activities of the plan or service are compatible with the lawyer's professional obligations. See Rule 5.3. Legal service plans and lawyer referral services may communicate with the public, but such communication must be in conformity with these rules. Thus, advertising must not be false or misleading, as would be the case if the communications of a group advertising program or a group legal services plan would mislead the public to think that it was a lawyer referral service sponsored by a state agency or bar association. Nor could the lawyer allow in-person, telephonic, or real-time contacts that would violate Rule 7.3.

[8]   [RESERVED]

Comparison to former Ohio Code of Professional Responsibility

Rule 7.2(a) directs attention to Rules 7.1 and 7.3, each of which includes or deletes language from the advertising and solicitation rules contained in DR 2-101 through DR 2-104.

The following are provisions of DR 2-101 that have not been included in Rule 7.1, 7.2, or 7.3:

- The specific reference to types of fees or descriptions, such as "give-away" or "below cost" found in DR 2-101(A)(5), although Rule 7.1, Comment [4] specifically indicates that these characterizations are misleading;

- Specific references to media types and words, as set forth in DR 2-101(B)(1) and (2);

- Specific reference that brochures or pamphlets can be disclosed to "others" as set forth in DR 2-101(B)(3);

- The list of items that were permissible for inclusion in advertising, contained in DR 2-101(D).

Comparison to ABA Model Rules of Professional Conduct

Rule 7.2(b)(3) is modified to remove a reference to a qualified legal referral service and substitute a reference to the lawyer referral service provisions contained in Rule XVI of the Supreme Court Rules for the Government of the Bar of Ohio. Rule 7.2 does not include Model Rule 7.2(b)(4) and thus prohibits reciprocal referral agreements between two lawyers or between a lawyer and a nonlawyer professional. Rule 7.2(d) is added to incorporate the prohibition contained in DR 2-101(A)(2) relative to soliciting employment where the lawyer does not intend to participate in the matter but instead will refer the matter to other counsel.

RULE 7.3: SOLICITATION OF CLIENTS

(a)   A lawyer shall not by in-person, live telephone, or real-time electronic contact solicit professional employment when a significant motive for the lawyer's doing so is the lawyer's pecuniary gain, unless either of the following applies:

(1)   the person contacted is a lawyer;

(2)   the person contacted has a family, close personal, or prior professional relationship with the lawyer.

(b)   A lawyer shall not solicit professional employment by *written*, recorded, or electronic communication or by in-person, telephone, or real-time electronic contact even when not otherwise prohibited by division (a), if any of the following applies:

(1)   the person being solicited has made *known* to the lawyer a desire not to be solicited by the lawyer;

(2)   the solicitation involves coercion, duress, or harassment;

(3)   the lawyer *knows* or *reasonably should know* that the person to whom the communication is addressed is a minor or an incompetent or that the person's physical, emotional, or mental state makes it unlikely that the person could exercise reasonable judgment in employing a lawyer.

(c)   Unless the recipient of the communication is a person specified in division (a)(1) or (2) of this rule, every *written*, recorded, or electronic communication from a lawyer soliciting professional employment from anyone whom the lawyer *reasonably believes* to be in need of legal services in a particular matter shall comply with all of the following:

(1)   Disclose accurately and fully the manner in which the lawyer or *law firm* became aware of the identity and specific legal need of the addressee;

(2)   Disclaim or refrain from expressing any predetermined evaluation of the merits of the addressee's case;

(3)   Conspicuously include in its text and on the outside envelope, if any, and at the beginning and ending of any recorded or electronic communication the recital - "ADVERTISING MATERIAL" or "ADVERTISEMENT ONLY."

(d)   Prior to making a communication soliciting professional employment pursuant to division (c) of this rule to a party who has been named as a defendant in a civil action, a lawyer or *law firm* shall verify that the party has been served with notice of the action filed against that party. Service shall be verified by consulting the docket of the court in which the action was filed to determine whether mail, personal, or residence service has been perfected or whether service by publication has been completed. Division (d) of this rule shall not apply to the solicitation of a debtor regarding representation of the debtor in a potential or actual bankruptcy action.

(e)   If a communication soliciting professional employment from anyone is sent within thirty days of an accident or disaster that gives rise to a potential claim for personal injury or wrongful death, the following "Understanding Your Rights" shall be included with the communication.

UNDERSTANDING YOUR RIGHTS*

If you have been in an accident, or a family member has been injured or killed in a crash or some other incident, you have many important decisions to make. It is important for you to consider the following:

1. Make and keep records - If your situation involves a motor vehicle crash, regardless of who may be at fault, it is helpful to obtain a copy of the police report, learn the identity of any witnesses, and obtain photographs of the scene, vehicles, and any visible injuries. Keep copies of receipts of all your expenses and medical care related to the incident.

2. You do not have to sign anything - You may not want to give an interview or recorded statement without first consulting with an attorney, because the statement can be used against you. If you may be at fault or have been charged with a traffic or other offense, it may be advisable to consult an attorney right away. However, if you have insurance, your insurance policy probably requires you to cooperate with your insurance company and to provide a statement to the company. If you fail to cooperate with your insurance company, it may void your coverage.

3. Your interests versus interests of insurance company - Your interests and those of the other person's insurance company are in conflict. Your interests may also be in conflict with your own insurance company. Even if you are not sure who is at fault, you should contact your own insurance company and advise the company of the incident to protect your insurance coverage.

4. There is a time limit to file an insurance claim - Legal rights, including filing a lawsuit, are subject to time limits. You should ask what time limits apply to your claim. You may need to act immediately to protect your rights.

5. Get it in *writing* - You may want to request that any offer of settlement from anyone be put in *writing*, including a *written* explanation of the type of damages which they are willing to cover.

6. Legal assistance may be appropriate - You may consult with an attorney before you sign any document or release of claims. A release may cut off all future rights against others, obligate you to repay past medical bills or disability benefits, or jeopardize future benefits. If your interests conflict with your own insurance company, you always have the right to discuss the matter with an attorney of your choice, which may be at your own expense.

7. How to find an attorney - If you need professional advice about a legal problem but do not know an attorney, you may wish to check with relatives, friends, neighbors, your employer, or co-workers who may be able to recommend an attorney. Your local bar association may have a lawyer referral service that can be found in the Yellow Pages or on the Internet.

8. Check a lawyer's qualifications - Before hiring any lawyer, you have the right to know the lawyer's background, training, and experience in dealing with cases similar to yours.

9. How much will it cost? - In deciding whether to hire a particular lawyer, you should discuss, and the lawyer's written fee agreement should reflect:

     a.   How is the lawyer to be paid? If you already have a settlement offer, how will that affect a contingent fee arrangement?

     b.   How are the expenses involved in your case, such as telephone calls, deposition costs, and fees for expert witnesses, to be paid? Will these costs be advanced by the lawyer or charged to you as they are incurred? Since you are obligated to pay all expenses even if you lose your case, how will payment be arranged?

     c.   Who will handle your case? If the case goes to trial, who will be the trial attorney?

This information is not intended as a complete description of your legal rights, but as a checklist of some of the important issues you should consider.

     *THE SUPREME COURT OF OHIO, WHICH GOVERNS THE CONDUCT OF LAWYERS IN THE STATE OF OHIO, NEITHER PROMOTES NOR PROHIBITS THE DIRECT SOLICITATION OF PERSONAL INJURY VICTIMS. THE COURT DOES REQUIRE THAT, IF SUCH A SOLICITATION IS MADE, IT MUST INCLUDE THE ABOVE DISCLOSURE.

     (f)   Notwithstanding the prohibitions in division (a) of this rule, a lawyer may participate with a prepaid or group legal service plan operated by an organization not owned or directed by the lawyer that uses in-person or telephone contact to solicit memberships or subscriptions for the plan from persons who are not *known* to need legal services in a particular matter covered by the plan.

Comment

[1]   A solicitation is a communication initiated by the lawyer that is directed to a specific person and that offers to provide, or can reasonably be understood as offering to provide, legal services. In contrast, a lawyer's communication typically does not constitute a solicitation if it is (a) directed to the general public, such as through a billboard, an Internet-based advertisement, a web site, or a commercial, (b) in response to a request for information, or (c) automatically generated in response to Internet searches.

[2]   There is a potential for abuse when a solicitation involves direct in-person, live telephone, or real-time electronic contact by a lawyer with someone known to need legal services. These forms of contact subject the person to the private importuning of the trained advocate in a direct interpersonal encounter. The person, who may already feel overwhelmed by the circumstances giving rise to the need for legal services, may find it difficult fully to evaluate all available alternatives with reasoned judgment and appropriate self-interest in the face of the lawyer's presence and insistence upon being retained immediately. The situation is fraught with the possibility of undue influence, intimidation, and over-reaching.

[3]   This potential for abuse inherent in direct in-person, live telephone, or real-time electronic solicitation justifies its prohibition, particularly since a lawyer has alternative means of conveying necessary information to those who may be in need of legal services. Communications can be mailed or transmitted by email or other electronic means that do not involve real-time contact and do not violate other laws governing solicitations. These forms of communication make it possible for the public to be informed about the need for legal services, and about the qualifications of available lawyers and law firms, without subjecting the public to direct in-person, telephone, or real-time electronic persuasion that may overwhelm the person's judgment. In using any telephone or other electronic communication, a lawyer remains subject to all applicable state and federal telemarketing laws and regulations.

[4]   The use of general advertising and written, recorded, or electronic communications to transmit information from lawyer to the public, rather than direct in-person, live telephone, or real-time electronic contact, will help to ensure that the information flows cleanly as well as freely. The contents of advertisements and communications permitted under Rule 7.2 can be permanently recorded so that they cannot be disputed and may be shared with others who know the lawyer. This potential for informal review is itself likely to help guard against statements and claims that might constitute false and misleading communications, in violation of Rule 7.1. The contents of direct in-person, live telephone, or real-time electronic contact can be disputed and may not be subject to third-party scrutiny. Consequently, they are much more likely to approach, and occasionally cross, the dividing line between accurate representations and those that are false and misleading.

[5]   There is far less likelihood that a lawyer would engage in abusive practices against a former client, a person with whom the lawyer has close personal or family relationship, or in situations in which the lawyer is motivated by considerations other than the lawyer's pecuniary gain. Nor is there a serious potential for abuse when the person contacted is a lawyer. Consequently, the general prohibition in Rule 7.3(a) and the requirements of Rule 7.3(c) are not applicable in those situations. Also, division (a) is not intended to prohibit a lawyer from

participating in constitutionally protected activities of public or charitable legal service organizations or bona fide political, social, civic, fraternal, employee, or trade organizations whose purposes include providing or recommending legal services to members or beneficiaries.

[6]   Even permitted forms of solicitation can be abused. Thus, any solicitation that contains information that is false or misleading within the meaning of Rule 7.1, that involves coercion, duress, or harassment within the meaning of Rule 7.3(b)(2), or that involves contact with someone who has made known to the lawyer a desire not to be solicited by the lawyer within the meaning of Rule 7.3(b)(1) is prohibited. Moreover, if after sending a letter or other communication as permitted by Rule 7.2 the lawyer receives no response, any further effort to communicate with the recipient may violate Rule 7.3(b).

[7]   This rule is not intended to prohibit a lawyer from contacting representatives of organizations or groups that may be interested in establishing a group or prepaid legal plan for their members, insureds, beneficiaries, or other third parties for the purpose of informing such entities of the availability of and details concerning the plan or arrangement that the lawyer or lawyer's firm is willing to offer. This form of communication is not directed to people who are seeking legal services for themselves. Rather, it is usually addressed to an individual acting in a fiduciary capacity seeking a supplier of legal services for others who may, if they choose, become prospective clients of the lawyer. Under these circumstances, the activity that the lawyer undertakes in communicating with such representatives and the type of information transmitted to the individual are functionally similar to and serve the same purpose as advertising permitted under Rule 7.2.

[8]   None of the requirements of Rule 7.3 applies to communications sent in response to requests from clients or others. General announcements by lawyers, including changes in personnel or office location, do not constitute communications soliciting professional employment from a person known to be in need of legal services within the meaning of this rule.

[8A]   The use of written, recorded, and electronic communications to solicit persons who have suffered personal injuries or the loss of a loved one can potentially be offensive. Nonetheless, it is recognized that such communications assist potential clients in not only making a meaningful determination about representation, but also can aid potential clients in recognizing issues that may be foreign to them. Accordingly, the information contained in division (e) must be communicated when the solicitation occurs within thirty days of an accident or disaster that gives rise to a potential claim for personal injury or wrongful death.

[9]   Division (f) of this rule permits a lawyer to participate with an organization that uses personal contact to solicit members for its group or prepaid legal service plan, provided that the personal contact is not undertaken by any lawyer who would be a provider of legal services through the plan. The organization must not be owned or directed, whether as manager or otherwise, by any lawyer or law firm that participates in the plan. For example, division (f) would not permit a lawyer to create an organization controlled directly or indirectly by the lawyer and use the organization for the in-person or telephone solicitation of legal employment of the lawyer through memberships in the plan or otherwise. The communication permitted by these organizations also must not be directed to a person known to need legal services in a particular matter, but is to be designed to inform potential plan members generally of another

means of affordable legal services. Lawyers who participate in a legal service plan must reasonably ensure that the plan sponsors are in compliance with Rules 7.1, 7.2, and 7.3(b). See Rule 8.4(a).

Comparison to former Ohio Code of Professional Responsibility

Rule 7.3 embraces the provisions of DR 2-104(A), DR 2-101(F) and DR 2-101(H), with modifications.

At division (c), the rule broadens the types of communications that are permitted by authorizing the use of recorded telephone messages and electronic communication via the Internet. Further, in keeping with the new methods of communication that are authorized, the provisions of DR 2-101(F) regarding disclosures are incorporated and modified to apply to all forms of permissible direct solicitations.

The provisions of DR 2-101(F)(2) have been incorporated in division (c) and modified to reduce the micromanagement of lawyer contact, which previously had been the subject of abuse, by requiring that the disclaimers "ADVERTISEMENT ONLY" and "ADVERTISING MATERIAL" be "conspicuously" displayed. The requirements contained in DR 2-101(F)(2)(b) regarding disclaimers of prior acquaintance or contact with the addressee and avoidance of personalization have not been retained.

The provisions of DR 2-101(F)(4) [pre-service solicitation of defendants in civil actions] have been inserted as a new division (d), and the provisions of DR 2-101(H) [solicitation of accident or disaster victims] have been inserted as a new division (e).

Comparison to ABA Model Rules of Professional Conduct

Rule 7.3 contains the following substantive changes to Model Rule 7.3:

- With the modifications discussed above, the requirements placed upon the lawyer involved in the direct solicitation of prospective clients are more stringent than the requirements contained in division (c) of the Model Rule. Because a lawyer is not likely to have actual knowledge [Rule 1.0(g)] of a prospective client's need for legal services, the Model Rule standard contained in division (c) is changed to "* * * soliciting professional employment from a prospective client whom the lawyer *reasonably believes* to be in need of legal services * * *." See Rule 1.0(j).

- Division (d), regarding preservice solicitation of defendants in civil actions, has been inserted.

- Division (e), regarding direct solicitation requirements respecting solicitation of accident or disaster victims and their families, has been inserted.

Added to the rule is Comment [7A], which discusses the rationale for inclusion of the new division (e).

APPENDIX B

OHIO ETHICS OPINION

The Supreme Court of Ohio

BOARD OF COMMISSIONERS ON GRIEVANCES & DISCIPLINE

65 SOUTH FRONT STREET, 5TH FLOOR, COLUMBUS, OH 43215-3431

Telephone: 614.387.9370

RICHARD A. DOVE
SECRETARY

Fax: 614.387.9379
www.supremecourt.ohio.gov

MICHELLE A. HALL
SENIOR COUNSEL

OPINION 2013-2
Issued April 5, 2013

Direct Contact with Prospective Clients: Text Messages

SYLLABUS: Prof.Cond.R. 7.2 allows lawyers to use text messages to solicit professional employment from prospective clients. However, text message solicitations must also comply with Prof.Cond.R. 7.1 and 7.3 and all applicable federal and state laws, rules, and regulations.

QUESTION PRESENTED: May Ohio lawyers use text messages to solicit professional employment from prospective clients?

APPLICABLE RULES: Rules 7.1, 7.2, and 7.3 of the Ohio Rules of Professional Conduct

OPINION:

Text Message Advertising is Generally Permissible under Prof.Cond.R. 7.2(a)

The Board has been asked to determine whether the Rules of Professional Conduct permit Ohio lawyers to advertise their services directly to prospective clients via text message. The technical term for "text messaging" is Short Message Service (SMS). Masur & Maher, *Mobile Phone Text Message Spam: Building a Vibrant Market for Mobile Advertising While Keeping Customers Happy*, 7 Va. Sports & Ent. L.J. 41, 44 (2007). "SMS text messaging systems allow users to write and send messages using the keypads or keyboards on their cell phones. Users can also send SMS text messages to and from email addresses or instant messaging applications directly to the recipient's mobile phone. However, the ability to send and receive SMS text messages is not always included in typical monthly cell phone plans. Many consumers pay additional monthly fees for text message allowances while other consumers are charged...for each SMS text

31

Op. 2013-2   2

message that they send or receive." *Id.* at 43-44. While SMS text messages are similar to e-mail messages in that both are electronic exchanges of text, SMS text messages are typically limited to 160 characters. *Id.* at 44. If a SMS text message is longer than 160 characters, some devices separate the message into multiple messages.

Text message technology is rapidly changing, and some companies provide "enhanced" messaging services that support messages more than 160 characters on certain devices. Also, Smartphone users can access internet text messaging applications ("apps") that are free and have greater character and image capacity.[1]

In the usual scenario reported to the Board, lawyers obtain the cellular phone numbers of prospective clients from accident or police reports. The lawyer then sends SMS text messages (hereinafter "text messages") directly to the cellular phone numbers indicated in the reports. The messages contain direct solicitations for professional employment. Given the limited number of characters usually available in a standard text message, the message contains very general information about the lawyer and his or her legal services. Often the message will contain an internet link to a website that contains additional advertising material.

Prof.Cond.R. 7.2(a) governs lawyer advertising and allows a broad range of marketing techniques within the constraints of the rules on general communication and direct contact with prospective clients. Prof.Cond.R. 7.2(a) states as follows:

> (a) Subject to the requirements of Rules 7.1 and 7.3, a lawyer may advertise services through written, recorded, or electronic communication, including public media.

"Electronic communication" is not defined in the Rules of Professional Conduct (Rules), but is generally understood to include text messages. *See, e.g.,* R.C. 4506.01(KK) and 4511.204(F). A text message could also be a "written

---

[1] Brian X. Chen, *Apps Redirect Text Messages, and Profits, from Cellular Providers* (Dec. 4, 2012), http://www.nytimes.com/2012/12/05/technology/free-messaging-apps-siphon-profits-from-cellular-providers.html (accessed Jan. 29, 2013).

communication" for purposes of Prof.Cond.R. 7.2 as " 'written' " denotes a tangible or electronic record of a communication or representation, including handwriting, typewriting, printing, photostating, photography, audio or videorecording, and e-mail." Prof.Cond.R. 1.0(p). The comments to Prof.Cond.R. 7.2 fail to reference text messages, but demonstrate that the Rules were drafted to take into account new or non-conventional advertising methods. For example, Comment [1] states that "[t]he interest in expanding public information about legal services ought to prevail over considerations of tradition." Comment [3] further states that "electronic media, such as the internet, can be an important source of information about legal services, and lawful communication by electronic mail is permitted by [Prof.Cond.R. 7.2]." Because text messages may be considered both an "electronic communication" and a "written communication" under the Rules of Professional Conduct, a plain reading of Prof.Cond.R. 7.2(a) indicates that lawyers may use text messages to advertise their services. This conclusion is consistent with the forward-thinking commentary to Prof.Cond.R. 7.2.

Text Message Advertising Must Otherwise Comply with Prof.Cond.R. 7.1-7.3

Although the Board finds that Prof.Cond.R. 7.2 allows text message advertising, further ethical guidance is required. As stated in Prof.Cond.R. 7.2(a), all lawyer advertising must comply with Prof.Cond.R. 7.1 and 7.3. There are also additional restrictions contained in Prof.Cond.R. 7.2 that apply to lawyer advertising. We will now separately examine these rules in the context of text message advertising by lawyers. Text messaging may be a novel approach to client solicitation, but our ethical review is actually a straightforward application of the Rules of Professional Conduct.

  a.   *False, Misleading, or Nonverifiable Communications*

Prof.Cond.R. 7.1 contains the general standard governing communications about a lawyer's services, and states as follows:

> A lawyer shall not make or use a false, misleading, or
> nonverifiable communication about the lawyer or the
> lawyer's services. A communication is false or
> misleading if it contains a material misrepresentation
> of fact or law or omits a fact necessary to make the

Op. 2013-2   4

statement considered as a whole not materially
misleading.

Prof.Cond.R. 7.1, Comment [1], verifies that lawyer advertising is a
"communication" under Prof.Cond.R. 7.1 and therefore subject to the prohibition
against false, misleading, and nonverifiable statements. Examples of statements
that may violate Prof.Cond.R. 7.1 are found in Comments [3], [4], and [5], and
include certain descriptions of past case results, unsubstantiated comparisons
with other lawyers, characterization of fees as "cut-rate," "lowest," "giveaway,"
"below cost," "discount," or "special," and statements concerning the ability to
improperly influence a government entity or official. Because text message
advertising of a lawyer's services must comply with Prof.Cond.R. 7.1, and is a
"communication" under that rule, such advertising cannot be false, misleading,
or contain nonverifiable information.

       b.   *Real-Time Electronic Contact*

       Prof.Cond.R. 7.2 also makes a lawyer's text message advertising subject to
Prof.Cond.R. 7.3, which restricts direct contact with prospective clients and
contains more detailed requirements than the general "false / misleading /
nonverifiable" standard contained in Prof.Cond.R. 7.1. Several of these
restrictions must be addressed in the context of text message advertising. First,
Prof.Cond.R. 7.3(a) prohibits live solicitation of prospective clients in most
situations:

> (a) A lawyer shall not by in-person, live telephone, or
> real-time electronic contact solicit professional
> employment from a prospective client when a
> significant motive for the lawyer's doing so is the
> lawyer's pecuniary gain, unless either of the
> following applies:
>> (1) the person contacted is a lawyer;
>> (2) the person contacted has a family, close
>> personal, or other professional relationship
>> with the lawyer.

The rationale for the prohibition against live solicitation is found in the
comments to Prof.Cond.R. 7.3, which state there is a "potential for abuse" when a
layperson is subject to the "private importuning of the trained advocate in a

Op. 2013-2   5

direct interpersonal encounter." Prof.Cond.R. 7.3, Comment [1]. Also, "the prospective client…may find it difficult fully to evaluate all available alternatives with reasoned judgment and appropriate self-interest in the face of the lawyer's presence and insistence upon being retained immediately." *Id.* A text message solicitation of a prospective client is not an in-person communication, and although it may be initiated with a cellular phone, would not ordinarily be considered a "live telephone" conversation. As we already determined that text messages are "electronic" communications for purposes of Prof.Cond.R. 7.2, to comply with Prof.Cond.R. 7.3(a), a text message solicitation of a prospective client cannot take place in "real-time."

Like Prof.Cond.R. 7.3(a), the American Bar Association's (ABA) Model Rule 7.3(a) also prohibits the solicitation of prospective clients by "real-time" electronic contact. The ABA has interpreted real-time electronic contact to include internet chat room communications. Bennett, Cohen & Whittaker, *Annotated Model Rules of Professional Conduct*, 553-554 (7th Ed. 2011). Chat rooms facilitate "live" text or voice conversations among multiple persons connected to the internet. The Board agrees that Prof.Cond.R. 7.3(a) prohibits lawyers from soliciting prospective clients via internet chat rooms as these are real-time electronic contacts. However, as stated in Prof.Cond.R. 7.2, Comment [3], lawyers are permitted to advertise by email. The Board's view is that a standard text message is more akin to an email than a chat room communication. Accordingly, a typical text message is not a "real-time" electronic contact. Lawyers may likewise solicit clients using test messages so long as the technology used to implement the text message does not generate a real-time or live conversation. [2]

    c.   *Coercion, Duress, or Harassment*

The next rule for lawyers to consider is Prof.Cond.R. 7.3(b), which states that lawyer solicitations are impermissible if the prospective client has requested that the lawyer not solicit them or the solicitation "involves coercion, duress, or harassment." Lawyers must honor the requests of prospective clients not to be solicited by text message or otherwise, and should refrain from additional

---

[2] "Voice texting" apps, for example, can be used to create real-time conversations that combine voice and text. *See* David Pogue, *Smartphone? Presto! 2-Way Radio* (Sept. 5, 2012), http://www.nytimes.com/2012/09/06/technology/personaltech/zello-heytell-and-voxer-make-your-smartphone-a-walkie-talkie-david-pogue.html (accessed Jan. 17, 2013).

solicitations if the prospective client does not respond. *See* Prof.Cond.R. 7.3, Comment [5]. Because most text messages are received on cellular phones, which are often carried on one's person, lawyers should be sensitive to the fact that a text message may be perceived as more invasive than an email.

      d.   *Persons in Need of Legal Services in a Particular Matter*

If a lawyer has a reasonable belief that a person is in need of legal services in a particular matter, Prof.Cond.R. 7.3(c) requires all written, recorded, or electronic solicitations to state how the lawyer became aware of the person and their legal needs, refrain from predetermined evaluations of the matter, and "conspicuously" include the words "ADVERTISING MATERIAL" or "ADVERTISEMENT ONLY" in the text, on the outside envelope, if any, and at the beginning and end of any "recorded or electronic communication." Unless a text message solicitation is sent to another lawyer, family member, or person with a close personal or prior professional relationship with the lawyer, the text message must comply with Prof.Cond.R. 7.3(c). Tracking the rule language, the text message must notify the recipient of the means by which the lawyer learned of the potential need for legal services, for example, from accident reports or a court docket, and include "ADVERTISING MATERIAL" or "ADVERTISEMENT ONLY" at both the beginning and ending of the message. These descriptors must be conspicuous and in capital letters as designated in the rule. The text message also cannot include an evaluation of the case or a prediction of the outcome.

The lawyer has an additional obligation if the prospective client to be solicited by text message is a defendant in a civil action. If so, Prof.Cond.R. 7.3(d) requires the lawyer to "verify that the [person] has been served with notice of the action...by consulting the court docket" before sending a text message solicitation. This requirement does not apply if the prospective client is a potential or actual bankruptcy debtor.

      e.   *Solicitation Within Thirty Days of Accident or Disaster*

The final content-based requirement of Prof.Cond.R. 7.3 is stated in division (e), which applies to lawyer solicitations sent to prospective clients or relatives of prospective clients within "thirty days of an accident or disaster that gives rise to a potential claim for personal injury or wrongful death." Prof.Cond.R. 7.3(e) mandates that the text of the "Understanding Your Rights"

Op. 2013-2   7

statement contained in the rule be "included with the communication." The "Understanding Your Rights" statement incorporates the following language: **"THE SUPREME COURT OF OHIO, WHICH GOVERNS THE CONDUCT OF LAWYERS IN THE STATE OF OHIO, NEITHER PROMOTES NOR PROHIBITS THE DIRECT SOLICITATION OF PERSONAL INJURY VICTIMS. THE COURT DOES REQUIRE THAT, IF SUCH A SOLICITATION IS MADE, IT MUST INCLUDE THE ABOVE DISCLOSURE."** (Emphasis in Prof.Cond.R. 7.3(e).)

Due to the limited number of characters available in a standard text message, including the entire "Understanding Your Rights" statement may cause the message to be split into multiple messages or fail to transmit in its entirety. Likely for this reason, some Ohio lawyers have included an internet link in their text message solicitations that allows the prospective client to view the "Understanding Your Rights" statement on the lawyer's website. In the Board's view, simply providing an internet link to the "Understanding Your Rights" statement does not comply with Prof.Cond.R. 7.3(e). Similarly, the Board believes that attachments or photographs containing the statement fail to satisfy Prof.Cond.R. 7.3(e). The rule requires that the statement be "included with the communication" and the Supreme Court's announcement at the end of the statement similarly indicates that the solicitation "must include" the statement. Comment [7A] also addresses the "Understanding Your Rights" statement, which "must be communicated to the prospective client or a relative of a prospective client." Given the language "included with the communication," "must include," and "must be communicated to," that the Supreme Court employed in Prof.Cond.R. 7.3(e) and Comment [7A], the Board concludes that the "Understanding Your Rights" statement must appear in the body of the lawyer's communication, and not as an internet link, attachment, photograph, or other item requiring additional action to access the statement. Although this may create multiple messages, it ensures that all recipients, regardless of the features on their cellular phones or service plans, have immediate access to the information. As with any solicitation sent to prospective clients within thirty days of an accident or disaster, the lawyer has the duty to ensure that the "Understanding Your Rights" statement is communicated to the text message recipient. Prof.Cond.R. 7.3, Comment [7A].

    f.   Identity of Lawyer or Law Firm Responsible for Content

Prof.Cond.R. 7.2, the general rule on lawyer advertising, contains two additional requirements that apply to text message solicitation of prospective clients. Prof.Cond.R. 7.2(c) states that "any communication made pursuant to this rule shall include the name and office address of at least one lawyer or law firm responsible for its content." Because text message advertising is a written or electronic communication made pursuant to Prof.Cond.R. 7.2, the text message must include the name and office address of the lawyer or law firm responsible for the message.

Also, Prof.Cond.R. 7.2(d) states that "[a] lawyer shall not seek employment in connection with a matter in which the lawyer or law firm does not intend to participate actively in the representation, but that the lawyer or law firm intends to refer to other counsel." As is the case with traditional prospective client solicitations, a lawyer may not seek employment via text message if the lawyer does not plan to participate in the representation.

Additional Considerations for Lawyers Employing Text Message Advertising

The Board has identified three practical considerations for a lawyer who chooses to directly solicit prospective clients using text messages. First, the text message should not create a cost to the prospective client. Not every cellular phone service plan includes free or unlimited text messaging, and significant costs may be incurred if the recipient is traveling internationally when the text is received. If the lawyer is unable to verify that a text message solicitation will not result in a cost to the prospective client, he or she should employ "Free to End User" or similar technology, by which the initiator of the text message is responsible for the cost of both delivery and receipt.

Second, the lawyer should be mindful of the age of the recipient of the text message. Minors are in possession of cellular phones in increasing numbers, and accident and police reports may contain cellular phone numbers that belong to minors. Such reports usually include dates of birth, and lawyers who obtain cellular phone numbers from such reports should attempt to verify that the numbers do not belong to minors before sending a text message solicitation. Although Prof.Cond.R. 7.3 does not explicitly prohibit the direct solicitation of

Op. 2013-2   9

minors as in some states, the Board discourages the solicitation of minors via text message.[3]

Finally, lawyers must use due diligence to ensure that any text message advertisement or solicitation complies with the applicable federal and state telemarketing laws. The Telephone Consumer Protection Act (TCPA) and the accompanying rules adopted by the Federal Communications Commission (FCC) prohibit a number of types of text messages sent by an autodialer to a cellular phone. *See* 47 U.S.C. 227; 47 C.F.R. 64.1200. Under new FCC regulations effective in 2012 and 2013, "prior express written consent for autodialed or prerecorded telemarketing calls to wireless numbers" is required and "all prerecorded telemarketing calls [must] allow consumers to opt out of future prerecorded telemarketing calls using an interactive, automated opt-out mechanism." 77 Fed. Reg. 112. Text messages are considered "calls" for purposes of the FCC rules. *See* 68 Fed. Reg. 143, ¶ 116; *Satterfield v. Simon & Schuster, Inc.*, 569 F.3d 946 (9th Cir. 2009). A lawyer's text message solicitation must also comply with the Controlling the Assault of Non-Solicited Pornography and Marketing Act (CAN-SPAM Act) and the accompanying rules adopted by the Federal Trade Commission (FTC). *See* 15 U.S.C. 7701-7713; 16 C.F.R. 316.1-316.6. The CAN-SPAM Act addresses unwanted email messages sent to cellular phones, which may appear as text messages. Further, lawyers are required to abide by federal "Do Not Call" provisions. *See* Prof.Cond.R. 7.3, Comment [2]; 15 U.S.C. 6151; 16 C.F.R. 310.4. Applicable state laws include R.C. 109.87, which authorizes the Ohio Attorney General to enforce the TCPA, and R.C. 2307.64, which regulates email advertisements. Before a lawyer engages in direct client solicitation by text message, the Board advises that the lawyer carefully scrutinize the message and delivery mechanism for compliance with all applicable federal and state laws, rules, and regulations.

CONCLUSION: Lawyers may advertise their services through SMS text messages, which are written and/or electronic communications for purposes of Prof.Cond.R. 7.2(a). All lawyer advertising, including text message advertising, must comply with Prof.Cond.R. 7.1 and 7.3. Under Prof.Cond.R. 7.1, the text message may not contain a false, misleading, or nonverifiable communication about the lawyer or the lawyer's services. Prof.Cond.R. 7.3 imposes five additional requirements that apply to text message advertising by lawyers:

---

[3] For references to state rules that regulate lawyers' direct solicitations of professional employment to minors, *see* Smolla, 1 Law of Lawyer Advertising 7:9 (Oct. 2012).

Op. 2013-2   10

- The text message cannot create a "real-time" interaction similar to an internet chat room;
- The text message may not involve coercion, duress, or harassment, and the lawyer must abide by a person's request not to receive solicitations;
- If the lawyer has a reasonable belief that the prospective client is in need of legal services in a particular matter, the text message must state how the lawyer learned of the need for legal services, include the language "ADVERTISING MATERIAL" OR "ADVERTISEMENT ONLY" at both the beginning and ending of the message, and cannot offer a case evaluation or prediction of outcome;
- If the prospective client is a defendant in a civil case, the lawyer shall verify that the person has been served; and
- Text message solicitations sent within 30 days of an accident or disaster must include, in the body of the text message, the entire "Understanding Your Rights" statement contained in Prof.Cond.R. 7.3(e).

In addition, under Prof.Cond.R. 7.2(c) and (d), the text message must include the name and address of the responsible lawyer or law firm and the lawyer may not solicit prospective clients if the lawyer does not intend to actively participate in the representation. The Board further recommends that lawyers employ "Free to End User" or other technology to avoid creating a cost to the text message recipient and attempt to verify that the text message recipient is not a minor. Finally, the Board advises lawyers to confirm that their text message advertising complies with all applicable federal and state laws, rules, and regulations, including the TCPA, CAN-SPAM Act, and Do Not Call Registry.

Advisory Opinions of the Board of Commissioners on Grievances and Discipline are informal, nonbinding opinions in response to prospective or hypothetical questions regarding the application of the Supreme Court Rules for the Government of the Bar of Ohio, the Supreme Court Rules for the Government of the Judiciary, the Ohio Rules of Professional Conduct, the Ohio Code of Judicial Conduct, and the Attorney's Oath of Office.

CHAPTER 2

ETHICS IN ELDER LAW REPRESENTATION

ISSUE AREAS

Clients with Diminished Capacity, Lawyer-Client Relationship, Confidentiality, Conflicts of Interest, Elder Law, Engagement Letters, Identifying the Client

---

LEARNING OBJECTIVES:

1. Analyze the ethical implications when a parent and child are involved in the retention of a lawyer for the purposes of the parent executing a will.

2. Consider the policies behind the qualification of for free legal service from a law school clinic.

3. Counsel clients and non-clients on legal and non-legal issues.

4. Determine who should be present during a client interview.

5. Draft an engagement letter for representation of a client in the execution of a will.

6. Explain what a lawyer can and should do, under the rules of professional conduct, when the lawyer believes the client suffers from diminished capacity.

7. Prepare a set of initial client intake questions.

8. Recognize best practices for preventing an undue influence challenge to a will.

BACKGROUND

This case study will help you better understand the unique issues that arise when lawyers represent clients who are guided by others, specifically, elder clients who are led by their children (or sometimes other caregivers) to pursue a particular course of legal action. These scenarios may present several ethical challenges for lawyers, including: who is the client, how to protect client confidential information and, in certain types of representation, how to avoid conflicts of interest.

Elder lawyers must know what to do if the client has, or the lawyer believes the client may have, diminished decision-making capacity that could affect the lawyer-client relationship or the legal representation. Elder law practitioners encounter these capacity issues more frequently than most other lawyers.[1] Therefore, elder law attorneys, and those who collaborate with and support these attorneys, must recognize the types of behavior indicative of diminished capacity, as well as how to respond consistent with the applicable rules of professional conduct.

The "normal client-lawyer relationship is based on the assumption that the client, when properly advised and assisted, is capable of making decisions about important matters."[2]

It is one where an autonomous client:

(1) has identified a problem as requiring the attention of a lawyer, (2) is capable of entering into an attorney-client (agent-principal) relationship, (3) will define the objectives of the relationship, (4) is responsible for the payment of any fees and costs, and (5) typically contacts and meets with the attorney unaccompanied or unassisted by others.[3]

As you work through this case study, first consider what aspects of the above described "normal" lawyer-client relationship are compromised or absent, if any. Then, determine under the applicable rules, and based on your personal moral compass, what actions a lawyer should take to ensure not only compliance with the relevant rules but also the best interests of the client.

Follow your intuition throughout this exercise. Consider how in this case, and in all the cases you will take as a lawyer, your knowledge of the relevant substantive law alone is necessary, but not sufficient, to wholly serve the client.

This case study will provide you with an opportunity to practice the following lawyering literacy skills: client counseling, factual investigation, oral and written communication, and reflective practice.

THE CASE STUDY

You are a law student in your school's Elder Law Clinic located in North Carolina. You take a phone call one day while the clinic staff and supervising attorney are out. A woman explains that she would like the clinic to help her father write a will. You explain that the clinic has certain

---

[1]   It is worth recognizing that as our population ages exponentially, it is important for all lawyers to understand the ins and outs of the ethical issues relating to client capacity. "The number of Americans ages 65 and older is projected to more than double from 46 million today to over 98 million by 2060, and the 65-and-older age group's share of the total population will rise to nearly 24 percent from 15 percent." Population Reference Bureau, *Fact Sheet: Aging in the United States, available at:* http://www.prb.org/Publications/Media-Guides/2016/aging-unitedstates-fact-sheet.aspx

It is also worth noting that capacity issues may arise due to factors other than advanced age, including traumatic brain injury, other cognitive impairment, and even youth, to name just a few.

[2]   North Carolina Rules of Professional Conduct, Comment 1 to Rule 1.14, *available at:* https://www.ncbar.gov/for-lawyers/ethics/rules-of-professional-conduct/rule-114-client-with-diminished-capacity/

[3]   A. Kimberley Dayton, Julie Ann Garber, Robert A. Mead, and Molly M. Wood, 1 ADVISING THE ELDERLY CLIENT § 3.2 (June 2017).

eligibility requirements regarding age, income, and residency, and that the first step is for the father, or the daughter with the father's permission, to complete an eligibility questionnaire. You give her the website with the questionnaire form. The daughter is frustrated, explaining that she only has access to the internet at the local library. She insists on bringing her father in and talking to someone in person, today.

PART ONE: THE PHONE CALL

1. Frequently, lawyers are faced with situations requiring them not to give legal advice but to counsel others, including clients, prospective clients, and even non-clients. This is one such time. How do you explain to the daughter that she or her father must complete the intake eligibility form to determine if he is eligible for legal representation by the clinic? How do you respond to her initial frustrations? Do you explain that she does not have to come with her father to the appointment? Why might you do so? How much of this conversation includes aspects of substantive legal knowledge? Be prepared to answer these questions and role play the phone call with your professors and classmates.

2. After further conversation, the daughter agrees to have her father complete the eligibility form. You receive the completed form via USPS mail several days later, and you and your supervising attorney agree that the father is eligible for the clinic's services.

    Legal aid offices, pro-bono providers, clinics, and other legal service providers who serve low-income clients have differing eligibility requirements. You will find a sample eligibility form from the Wake Forest School of Law Elder Law Clinic here: http://elder-clinic.law.wfu.edu/services/new-client-questionnaire/. What do you think about the income requirements for qualifying for services? What do you think about the disclaimer regarding confidential information and the lawyer-client relationship? Would you revise either of these? Be prepared to discuss these questions in class and provide specific suggestions for any improvements you believe should be made.

PART TWO: THE CLIENT INTAKE

1. You call the father and schedule the interview for next week. Your supervising attorney explains that she would like you to take the lead on the interview. You recall from the phone call with the daughter, and from the completed eligibility questionnaire, that the legal issue for which the father seeks assistance is "writing a will." Draft a set of interview questions. (Do not worry if you haven't taken a course yet in trusts and estates or will-making. You do not need to include substantive questions about the content of the will itself.)

2. The following week, the father and the daughter arrive for the interview. You are surprised to see the daughter. You had advised her

that her presence was not necessary. Your supervising attorney advises that the interview must be conducted without the daughter's presence. Why?

> **HINT:** As you begin to consider the unique issues that may arise from this representation, review the National Academy of Elder Law Attorneys Aspirational Standards for the representation of elderly clients. Consider these standards as you think about why you may want to interview the father alone and as you work through the remainder of this case study.
>
> https://www.naela.org/Web/About_Tab/History_and_Standards/ History_and_Standards_Sub_landing/Aspirational_Standards.aspx

3. You decide to take an approach modeled by your supervising attorney in previous interviews. You explain to the father and the daughter you would like to talk with the father first, without the daughter present. What words do you use?

4. Immediately, the daughter is eager to talk for her father, saying that her presence in the interview is necessary. "Daddy can't explain himself so well." She quickly explains that while she has two brothers who live out of state,

> Daddy wants me to have the house, because I've been taking care of him since Mama died. He does not want my good for nothing brothers to get it.

How do you respond? How do you respond if the father says, "It's okay; let her join us?" What if he says, "I want my daughter present in the interview?"

You know from your Professional Responsibility course and your experience in the clinic that the father is the client, not the daughter. How do you explain this to the daughter and to her father? Remember, you are in the waiting room with both of them (and your supervising attorney). Be prepared to role play with your professors and classmates.

As you prepare, consider these questions: (1) what obligations does a lawyer have regarding confidential client information; (2) what conflicts of interest might arise in this representation; and (3) what risks to the representation and to you exist if the daughter is pressuring the father?

> **HINT:** Review the relevant North Carolina Rules of Professional Conduct (Rules 1.6, 1.7, and 1.8). Can you find them on the North Carolina State Bar's homepage?
>
> https://www.ncbar.gov/

> **HINT:** You know from the Aspirational Standards why interviewing the father alone is important; the issue is how to explain this while respecting the father and the daughter and also complying with your ethical obligations. Review the brochure "Why Am I Left in the Waiting Room," which explains to the daughter what is happening and why. What tips can you get from this document?
>
> http://elder-clinic.law.wfu.edu/files/2013/05/Four-Cs.pdf

> **HINT:** You might also review Section II of the following: Rebecca C. Morgan, *Who is the Client? Ethical Issues in an Elder Law Practice*, Journal of American Academy of Matrimonial Lawyers (2000), *available at:*
>
> http://sc.aaml.org/sites/default/files/who%20is%20the%20client%20 ethical%20issues-16-2.pdf

5. The father and the daughter agree that you and your supervising attorney may conduct the interview outside of the daughter's presence. You begin by asking the father questions about his home and his desire to leave the house to the daughter. You ask about his sons. The conversation goes like this:

You:	So, tell me why you are here today.
Client Father:	Well, my daughter thinks I need a will.
You:	Do you think you need a will?
Client Father:	Maybe. She has been really good to me since my wife died. My good for nothing boys might take the house from her.
You:	Who is her?
Client Father:	My daughter. She wants my house.
You:	What do you want?
Client Father:	I want my daughter to be happy. I want to take care of her.

You are acutely aware that if the father is being pressured by the daughter to leave her his home, the will may be challenged, perhaps successfully, at a later date based on undue influence. Undue influence is one individual pressuring another to take an action that has legal consequences: in this case, executing the will. Your concern is that after the father's death, the sons (or some other individual) will argue that this was not the father's actual intent.

Based on your observations thus far, what steps should you take at this point to ensure that you are representing the father's wishes and that an undue influence challenge is unlikely to succeed?

> **HINT:** Courts generally analyze four elements in determining whether there is undue influence. While state law varies (and the specifics are beyond the scope of this case study), what you should understand is that undue influence requires four elements: "(1) a person who is subject to influence; (2) a disposition to exert undue influence; (3) an opportunity to exert undue influence; and (4) a result indicating undue influence."[4]
>
> Taking these factors into account, what best practices should you consider?

> **HINT:** Your clinic supervisor tells you that she likes to "encourage and ask the hard questions, using plain language." Think about this as you consider the steps you should take. Consider how you, in your everyday life, talk with elderly family and friends, or how you explain things to those who do not have the legal understanding that you have.

PART THREE: THE ENGAGEMENT LETTER

1. After further conversation with the father, you are clear about the purposes of the representation and confident, because you have followed best practices, that executing a will leaving the home to the daughter is in accordance with the father's intent. You tell the father that you will follow up with an engagement letter, detailing what you have talked about. You explain you will mail this to him within two business days. You return to the waiting room to meet the daughter and say your goodbyes. Draft this engagement letter.

> **HINT:** Review the template agreement in Appendix A. Use this example to draft your engagement letter.

PART FOUR: A SLIGHT CHANGE OF FACTS

1. The above scenario presented several potential ethics issues. It does not present an issue that elder lawyers commonly encounter: diminished capacity. Remember, the "normal client-lawyer relationship is based on the assumption that the client, when properly advised and assisted, is capable of making decisions about important

---

4   Richard B. Keeton, *Balancing Testamentary Incapacity and Undue Influence: How to Handle Will Contests of Testators With Diminishing Capacity*, 57 S. TEX. L REV. 53, 67 (2015).

matters."[5] If the client's ability to make such decisions is impaired, the representation may be undermined in a number of ways, including exposing the client's documents to legal challenges that could have been avoided. Assume that during the interview with the father, you and your supervising attorney develop concerns that he may lack the capacity to write the will. What do you do?

> **HINT:** Review North Carolina Rule of Professional Conduct 1.14 and the comments. Remember, you may find them on the North Carolina State Bar's homepage. https://www.ncbar.gov/ Also, review the *"What If You Become Mentally Unable to Manage Your Affairs?"* document at Appendix B.

DOCUMENTS USED IN THE CASE STUDY

Appendix A: Form Engagement Letter[6]

Appendix B: *What If You Become Mentally Unable to Manage Your Affairs?* Client Handout[7]

---

[5]   North Carolina Rules of Professional Conduct, Comment 1 to Rule 1.14, *available at* https://www.ncbar.gov/for-lawyers/ethics/rules-of-professional-conduct/rule-114-client-with-diminished-capacity/.

[6]   Reprinted with permission of the Wake Forest University School of Law Elder Law Clinic.

[7]   Reprinted with permission of the Wake Forest University School of Law Elder Law Clinic.

FORM ENGAGEMENT LETTER

Date

[Client's name
and address]
City, State, Zip

Dear Mr./Mrs. _____:

It was a pleasure meeting with you. This letter is to confirm that The Elder Law Clinic has agreed to [state agreed upon work; ex.: draft a will, living will, health care power of attorney, power of attorney, and a medical information release form; advise you about Medicaid; advise you about your problem with (name of opposing party)].

[Use if applicable]: You indicated that this office could release any information you provided me to [state name and relationship of person(s); ex.: your daughter, D.D. Jones], if I determine that this would be in your best interests.

On occasion, our clients become ill while we are representing them. I am enclosing a page that explains how we would handle such a situation if that were to happen to you. Please let me know if you have questions about it. [Do not use if Clinic is representing guardian or other fiduciary on behalf of incompetent older person]

[Include for married couple seeking Medicaid planning:] It is my understanding that you both want me to advise you about preserving your assets if one spouse becomes ill and needs nursing home care. Also, you are aware that such a plan generally will provide for some or all of your property to be shifted to the healthy spouse, taking property out of the name of the ill spouse. This may be legally disadvantageous to the ill spouse.

*[Include for married couple for whom you are doing **wills; remove italics:** This letter is also to confirm that The Elder Law Clinic is representing **both** of you in preparing your estate plan. We have talked about the chance that representing **both** of you might lead to a "conflict of interest" for the Clinic at some later time. A "conflict of interest" means that what may be best for one spouse might **not** be best for the other.*

If, in the future, the Clinic determines that your interests are in conflict and that we cannot adequately represent both of you, then the Clinic may need to withdraw from representing either of you.

*Also, I have explained to you that ordinarily an attorney is required to keep a client's communications private, even from the client's spouse. This is called the "attorney-client privilege." You both have agreed to waive or give up the attorney-client privilege. As a result, I will **not** be required to* *keep what you have told me confidential from your spouse. If one of you tells me something that is important for the other spouse to know, I will reveal this information to the other spouse.*

This waiver of confidentiality, however, is only with respect to information between the Clinic and you both. We will still keep everything you tell us confidential with respect to third parties.

Of course, each of you is free to consult or switch to a lawyer from another law firm at any time, despite your decision now to have me represent you.]

OPTIONAL PARAGRAPHS RE DPOA:

Here is some information about the Durable Power of Attorney. As the "Principal"—the person signing the document—you are using this Durable Power of Attorney to grant power to another person (called the "agent" or "attorney-in-fact"). That person will be able to make decisions concerning your money and property, on your behalf. If this Durable Power of Attorney does not limit the powers that you give your Agent, your Agent will have broad and sweeping powers to sell or otherwise dispose of your property, and to spend your money without advance notice to you or approval by you.

Under this document, your Agent will continue to have these powers after you become incapacitated, and unless otherwise indicated, your Agent will have these powers before you become incapacitated.

You have the right to revoke or take back this Durable Power of Attorney at any time, so long as you are of sound mind. We will talk about this when you return here.

In addition, if you have an investment account or other account with a financial institution, I suggest that you ask them about their own "power of attorney" form. Some institutions prefer that a customer use their "in-house" form in addition to the power of attorney form that we will prepare for you.

[As I stated in our interview, we will not be able to help you with [   ], nor does The Elder Law Clinic have an opinion about the validity of these claims. Other counsel should be sought if you have questions regarding these issues.]

I look forward to seeing you again at our appointment on [date] at [time]. If you have any questions, please feel free to call.

Sincerely,

Your name
Certified Law Student
Under the Supervision of
Managing Attorney

Encl.

APPENDIX B

WHAT IF YOU BECOME MENTALLY UNABLE TO MANAGE YOUR AFFAIRS? CLIENT HANDOUT

WHAT IF YOU BECOME MENTALLY UNABLE TO MANAGE YOUR AFFAIRS?

This page explains our policy if we have serious concerns about your mental capacity.

If we are still representing you, we will continue to do so. We will take steps to protect your interests. We will follow legal standards of practice and ethics rules. N.C. ethics rules provide that, when a client cannot act in his own interest, the lawyer may take appropriate action in assessing the client's capacity and considering protective action. This could include seeking appointment of a guardian.

I would only take actions that I reasonably believe to be in your best interests and consistent with your previously expressed wishes.

Unless you direct me otherwise in writing, you authorize me:

(1) to communicate with your family, your physicians and your other advisors and to give them confidential (private) information that I think is appropriate under the circumstances, and

(2) to represent one or more members of your family or other advisors acting in a fiduciary relationship (which means a "trusted" relationship) for your or your property. However, I would not represent them in any proceeding involving determination of your capacity.

Please tell me if you have questions or concerns about this. Thank you.

The reason is simple (though sometimes debated): trust is the "hallmark of the client-lawyer relationship." Only when a client trusts her lawyer will she feel as though she can disclose the information necessary for the lawyer to provide effective representation. Without all relevant information, the representation will be limited; when confidentiality is protected, the client can rest assured that she can tell the lawyer and the lawyer will protect even embarrassing or legally harmful information.

Every state provides for the protection of client confidential information. And, every state provides exceptions to the general rule against lawyer disclosure, even though *any* exception necessarily risks eroding the trust that is so fundamental to the lawyer-client relationship and, therefore, the representation.

The most basic exceptions are when: (1) the lawyer has the client's informed consent to disclose the information; and (2) the disclosure is impliedly authorized. There is little risk to the client's trust in these situations. In the first, the client has consented and, in the second, the disclosure is permitted to carry out the representation for which the client hired the lawyer.

However, most states also permit lawyers to disclose confidential information when:

(1) the lawyer reasonably believes another person is at risk of substantial bodily harm or death;

(2) the client is using the lawyer's services, or has used the services, in a way that harms another financially;

(3) the lawyer needs advice on complying with the rules of professional conduct;

(4) the lawyer needs to establish a claim or defense against the client regarding the representation; and

(5) other laws or a court order permits disclosure.

Some states also permit disclosure when a lawyer is changing jobs.

Consider what this means: each of the above-listed exceptions represents a scenario where a lawyer, *without* the client's consent, may disclose confidential client information. Despite what may seem like a long list of exceptions, there are still many instances when lawyers are not permitted to disclose, even though it may seem they should be allowed to disclose. For example, in nearly all jurisdictions, if a lawyer learns confidentially from a client that someone has been wrongfully convicted of a crime and has been incarcerated, the lawyer is not allowed to disclose this information.

Two especially high-profile cases highlight the tensions this can create for the lawyer and the larger impact on individuals, as well as on our justice system and society's perception of our system.

- Lee Wayne Hunt and Jerry Cashwell were each convicted of murdering two individuals in rural North Carolina. After nearly twenty years in prison, Mr. Cashwell committed suicide; his lawyer then came forward and said that Mr. Cashwell told him from the start of the representation that Mr. Cashwell alone committed the murders and that Mr. Hunt was, in fact, innocent.[1]

- Alton Logan served 26 years in prison for a murder at a Chicago McDonalds. He was released after two lawyers for another man came forward and revealed that their deceased client, prior to his death, had confessed to the murder. The lawyers had known since Mr. Logan's conviction that he was innocent; however, their client would not permit them to come forward until after his death.[2]

Each of the lawyers involved in these cases followed the relevant state ethics rules governing lawyer conduct when they refused to disclose that these wrongfully convicted men were in fact innocent. Each of these lawyers subsequently faced public and professional repercussions. However, their eventual disclosure of innocence had very different outcomes because of the actions they took prior to the disclosures.

The two lawyers whose admission eventually freed Mr. Logan obtained consent from their client to disclose their client's guilt after his death. You should recognize immediately that this consent was necessary to comply with the rules, because the lawyer's duty of confidentiality continues after death. In addition, the two lawyers had their client waive the attorney-client privilege. Why? Privilege also survives the death of a client, and without this waiver, it is possible that their client's information would not have been admissible in court.

In other words, even if the lawyers had their client's consent and therefore were not violating the professional conduct rules when they disclosed, without this waiver of attorney-client privilege, a judge may have refused to admit their testimony in court and therefore precluded Mr. Logan's release.

In the second case, the lawyer for Mr. Cashwell, who disclosed Mr. Hunt's innocence, did not obtain such consent. In fact, when the lawyer testified in a hearing requesting a new trial for Mr. Hunt, the judge said "[i]f you testify, I will be compelled to report you to the state bar." The lawyer replied that he had

---

[1]   *See* Adam Besley, *When Innocence Is Confidential: A New and Essential Exception to Attorney-Client Confidentiality*, 56 SANTA CLARA L. REV. 147 (2016); *see also* Colin Miller, *Ordeal by Innocence: Why There Should Be A Wrongful Incarceration/Execution Exception to Attorney-Client Confidentiality*, 102 NW. U.L. REV. COLLOQUY 391, 393 (2008).

[2]   Besley, *supra* note 1.

never, ever, ever before violated a client's confidence . . . [b]ut [my client is] dead. My disclosure can't hurt him[,] and I have to weigh that disclosure against the continuing harm [to Mr. Hunt].[3]

A disciplinary complaint was filed against the lawyer, but the North Carolina State Bar dismissed it in a confidential decision.[4] Mr. Hunt remains in prison (as of the time of this publication).

What do you think *should* be the outcome in these cases? Should the hallmark of trust preclude the disclosure of client confidential information, even in cases of wrongful conviction, or should there be additional exceptions to permit disclosure in these situations? What are the pros and cons of exceptions to the general confidentiality rules?

This case study will allow you to explore these questions, while practicing the following lawyering literacy skills: client counseling, legal problem solving, legal reasoning, policymaking and legal reform, research, and oral and written communication.

THE CASE STUDY

You are a third-year law student participating in your school's Innocence & Justice Clinic, which is modeled after the Innocence Project.[5] As you learn more about criminal justice reform and ways to prevent wrongful incarceration, you question why, from a policy standpoint, a lawyer who knows that an innocent person is wrongfully incarcerated may be unable to tell anyone. You are alarmed that there are seven exceptions to the general rule of confidentiality, but not one exception requires—or even permits—disclosure when a lawyer knows an innocent person is serving a prison sentence. You ask your clinic professor for guidance on how you can better familiarize yourself with this issue and advocate for reform.

PART ONE: WHAT DO THE RULES OF PROFESSIONAL CONDUCT PROVIDE?

1. You start by analyzing the state of the rules today. You've heard your clinic professor say that such disclosure would not be permitted under the rules of your law school's home state, New York. But you decide to double check. What do you find? For this and all other questions in this case study, use the hints below only if you have difficulties after searching on your own.

---

[3] Adam Liptak, *When Law Prevents Righting a Wrong*, N.Y. TIMES (May 4, 2008), Week in Review, *available at* http://www.nytimes.com/2008/05/04/weekinreview/04liptak.html.

[4] *Id.*

[5] https://www.innocenceproject.org/about/.

> **HINT:** Explore the New York State Unified Court System website and search the New York Rules of Professional Conduct:
>
> http://www.nycourts.gov/rules/jointappellate/index.shtml
>
> Was your professor correct?

2. You recall from your Professional Responsibility course that many states follow the Model Rules of Professional Conduct. Is the result under the Model Rules the same as in New York?

> **HINT:** Recall the ABA's website for the Model Rules:
>
> https://www.americanbar.org/groups/professional_responsibility/ publications/model_rules_of_professional_conduct/model_rules_of_ professional_conduct_table_of_contents.html

3. You wonder if the result is the same in every state. Your professor tells you that Alaska, and perhaps Massachusetts, have revised their professional conduct rules to permit lawyers to disclose confidential client information when they believe someone is wrongly incarcerated. Find the relevant rule in these jurisdictions. How do these rules differ from New York with respect to disclosure of wrongful convictions? What do you think are the pros and cons to the approaches these jurisdictions have taken?

> **HINT:** Most states' rules of professional conduct may be found online. Can you find them on the Alaska Bar Association's website?
>
> https://alaskabar.org/
>
> In Massachusetts, the rules can be found on the Supreme Judicial Court's website:
>
> http://www.mass.gov/courts/case-legal-res/rules-of-court/sjc/sjc307. html

> **YOUR HOMETOWN:** Now conduct the same searches for your hometown. Would such disclosure of confidential client information be allowed under the rules in your state? What about the state in which you plan to practice law?

4. Is it possible that in the states without explicit exceptions like Alaska and Massachusetts, wrongful incarceration may constitute "substantial bodily harm" or "reasonably certain death?" Consider the arguments in favor of and against wrongful incarceration constituting "substantial bodily harm" and "reasonably certain death," and come to class prepared to defend your positions.

> **LEARN MORE:** Others have considered these arguments as well. *See, e.g.*, Colin Miller, *Ordeal by Innocence: Why There Should Be A Wrongful Incarceration Exception to Attorney-Client Confidentiality*, 102 N.W. L. REV. COLLOQUY 391, 395–99 (2008), *available at:* https://scholarlycommons.law.northwestern.edu/nulr_online/121/; Restatement (Third) of the Law Governing Lawyers, § 66, cmt. c (2000).

PART TWO: REVISIONS TO THE NEW YORK RULE

1. You ask your clinic professor about the process for revising the rules. Your professor explains that each state has its own process; but generally, the rules are promulgated by the courts. In New York, the Rules of Professional Conduct are adopted by the Appellate Division of the New York State Supreme Court and codified at 22 NYCRR Part 1200. Your professor explains that in adopting these rules, the court seeks input from designated committees, the legal community, and the public.

    In fact, your clinic professor is working with a group of innocence clinics throughout the state to advocate for reform in New York. They plan to make recommendations to the Committee on Standards of Attorney Conduct for the New York State Bar Association, which is "charged with monitoring and evaluating the New York Code of Professional Responsibility (Rules of Model Conduct) and other provisions that regulate lawyers and the practice of law in New York State." (http://www.nysba.org/A16900/). Your professor explains that the group has been investigating various revisions to the New York Rules to permit disclosure of confidential information in cases of wrongful conviction, like those of Alton Logan and Lee Wayne Hunt. They are considering three possible amendments to the New York Rules of Professional Conduct Rule 1.6. Your professor asks you to draft a summary of the pros and cons of each of the following three proposed amendments.

    Proposed Amendment One (The redlines represent the changes to the current New York Rule 1.6.)

    (b)   A lawyer may reveal or use confidential information to the extent that the lawyer reasonably believes necessary:

    >   (1)   to prevent reasonably certain death, or substantial bodily harm, or wrongful execution or incarceration of another;

    >   (2)   to prevent the client from committing a crime;

    >   (3)   to withdraw a written or oral opinion or representation previously given by the lawyer and reasonably believed by the lawyer still to be relied upon by a third person, where the lawyer has discovered that the opinion or representation was based on

materially inaccurate information or is being used to further a crime or fraud;

(4) to secure legal advice about compliance with these Rules or other law by the lawyer, another lawyer associated with the lawyer's firm or the law firm;

(5)(i) to defend the lawyer or the lawyer's employees and associates against an accusation of wrongful conduct; or (ii) to establish or collect a fee; or

(6) when permitted or required under these Rules or to comply with other law or court order.

Proposed Amendment Two

The Following Unnumbered Paragraph should be included in New York Rule 1.6(b), following Rule 1.6(b)(6):

This rule does not prohibit a lawyer from revealing or using confidential information, to the extent that the lawyer reasonably believes necessary, to prevent or rectify the conviction of another person for an offense that the lawyer reasonably believes the other person did not commit, where the client to whom the confidential information relates is deceased.

Proposed Amendment Three (The redlines represent the changes to the current New York Rule 1.6.)

(b) A lawyer may reveal, and must reveal in subsection (7), or use confidential information to the extent that the lawyer reasonably believes necessary:

(1) to prevent reasonably certain death or substantial bodily harm;

(2) to prevent the client from committing a crime;

(3) to withdraw a written or oral opinion or representation previously given by the lawyer and reasonably believed by the lawyer still to be relied upon by a third person, where the lawyer has discovered that the opinion or representation was based on materially inaccurate information or is being used to further a crime or fraud;

(4) to secure legal advice about compliance with these Rules or other law by the lawyer, another lawyer associated with the lawyer's firm or the law firm;

(5)(i) to defend the lawyer or the lawyer's employees and associates against an accusation of wrongful conduct; or (ii) to establish or collect a fee; or

(6) when permitted or required under these Rules or to comply with other law or court order; or

(7) to rectify the wrongful execution or incarceration of another; a person whose information is revealed in this manner is granted use immunity for the information provided.

In analyzing these three proposals, consider the following: whether disclosure should be permitted after the death of the client; whether the disclosure should be permissive or mandatory; what harm might come to the profession from such disclosures; and what are the pros and cons for the lawyer who knows such information. Determine which proposal is the best option and why; be ready to explain your choice.

> **HINT:** Start by analyzing and detailing the differences in each of the three amendments. Then, consider your thoughts on the pros and cons of each. Review any commentary you can find on the Alaska and Massachusetts Rules, as well as the following articles:
>
> (1) New York City Bar, Proposed Amendment to Rule of Professional Conduct 1.6—Authorizing Disclosure of Confidential Information of Deceased Clients, *available at*:
>
> http://www.nycbar.org/pdf/report/uploads/20071914-Proposed AmendmenttoRuleofProfessionalConduct1.6.pdf
>
> (2) Adam Belsey, *When Innocence Is Confidential: A New and Essential Exception to Attorney-Client Confidentiality*, 56 SANTA CLARA L. REV. 147 (2016), *available at:*
>
> https://digitalcommons.law.scu.edu/lawreview/vol56/iss1/4/

2. Based on the samples above, and on your research and analysis of these proposed amendments, determine the best strategy for adding such an exception in your hometown jurisdiction or in the jurisdiction in which you plan to practice. Begin by reviewing the relevant rules. Then draft an exception to permit disclosure in cases of wrongful conviction in the jurisdiction.

PART THREE: WHAT ABOUT THE ATTORNEY-CLIENT PRIVILEGE?

1. You recognize from your Professional Responsibility and Evidence courses that even if an exception to the rules exists to permit the disclosure of such confidential client information, there is still an issue if the information is protected by the attorney-client privilege. Under what circumstances would the information be privileged?

> **HINT:** You can find the elements of the attorney-client privilege in the Restatement (Third) of the Law Governing Lawyers § 68 (2000).

2. What if the information the lawyer learns about the wrongful conviction *is* attorney-client privileged? Even if the lawyer is permitted to disclose under the relevant rules of professional conduct, the privileged information may not be admitted in court, unless the client waives the privilege. Why? Remember: the privilege belongs to the client; generally, only the client can the waive the privilege. Put yourself in the shoes of the man who confessed to his lawyers that Alton Logan was innocent, and that he, in fact, committed the crime. Assume your client refuses to let you disclose his confession until after his death. You have consent under Rule 1.6, but what do you do to ensure a proper waiver of the privilege? Draft such a waiver. Be sure to consider the scope and timing of the waiver. Then consider how you would counsel your client to ensure that the client understands the consequences of signing the waiver.

> **HINT:** See the sample waiver in Appendix A.

PART FOUR: AN ALTERNATIVE APPROACH

1. Very recently, North Carolina adopted a different, unique approach for handling these issues. This provision can be found at North Carolina Rule of Professional Conduct Rule 8.6. Find this rule.

> **HINT:** You can locate the North Carolina Rules of Professional Conduct here:
>
> https://www.ncbar.gov/for-lawyers/ethics/rules-of-professional-conduct/rule-86-information-about-a-possible-wrongful-conviction/

2. How is the North Carolina Rule different from the three approaches above? What is the relationship of Rule 1.6 to this Rule? Does North Carolina need an exception to Rule 1.6 like those above given the existence of Rule 8.6? Do lawyers have the same issues with privileged information as they do in states like Alaska and Massachusetts that have an express exception to Rule 1.6 for wrongful convictions?

> **LEARN MORE:** Review the following article: David L. Hudson, *Some states now require all attorneys to report wrongful conduct*, ABA JOURNAL, September 2017, *available at:*
>
> http://www.abajournal.com/magazine/article/wrongful_convictions_legal_ethics_hudson

DOCUMENTS USED IN THE CASE STUDY

Appendix A: Form Release of Attorney-Client Privilege

APPENDIX A

FORM RELEASE OF ATTORNEY-CLIENT PRIVILEGE

This will authorize the release, by Law Firm, LLC, of certain attorney-client privileged information. The undersigned client authorizes the release and disclosure by Law Firm, LLC of the privileged information detailed below.

I permit the lawyers at Law Firm, LLC to communicate about [____] with the following people: [____]

I expressly waive the attorney-client privilege as to the above information and records only as to Law Firm, LLC and its representatives.

I have had an opportunity to discuss this release with my attorney and I am knowingly, intelligently, and voluntarily releasing Law Firm, LLC to [____] with [____].

I understand that this release may be withdrawn by at any time by submitted such withdrawal in writing to Law Firm, LLC.

Date:

Client Signature:

Client Name Printed:

Approved by:

For Law Firm, LLC

CHAPTER 4

WAIVING A CONFLICT OF INTEREST BEFORE IT ARISES

ISSUE AREAS:

Advance Waivers of Conflicts, Conflicts of Interest, Engagement Letters, Informed Consent, Lawyer Disqualification

LEARNING OBJECTIVES:

1. Analyze advance waiver of conflicts of interest for validity under the applicable rules governing lawyers.

2. Consider the policy reasons in favor of and against the use of advance waivers.

3. Determine what constitutes proper informed consent under the applicable rules governing lawyers.

4. Draft an advance waiver of future conflicts of interest.

5. Evaluate the use of advance conflicts waivers in the practice of law.

6. Identify best practices for the use of advance waivers in today's legal market.

7. Locate the applicable rules governing lawyers' use of advance waivers in a given jurisdiction.

8. Recognize the consequences of representing clients who have conflicts of interest, absent a valid waiver.

BACKGROUND

This case study will expand your understanding of conflicts of interest and allow you to explore what constitutes informed consent to conflicts of interest by examining when clients may consent to conflicts *before* they arise. Recall that the rules prohibiting representation when a conflict of interest exists are designed to protect the client; these rules are based on the duty of loyalty, which every lawyer equally owes every client.

Because of this duty of loyalty, professional conduct rules prohibit lawyers from representing clients when the parties are directly adverse, or when the lawyer's ability to represent each client will be materially limited in some way, unless the conflict of interest is consentable, and the lawyer gets *proper* consent from *each* client. *See* Model Rule of Professional Conduct 1.7.

Conflicts of interest are consentable when: (1) the lawyer reasonably believes that the lawyer can adequately protect the interests of each client; (2) the representation is not prohibited by law; and (3) the parties involved are not aligned against one another in a tribunal. If each of these is satisfied, the lawyer must then obtain consent.

But, what makes consent to the conflict of interest proper? First, it must be in writing; that's the easy part. More challenging is that the consent must be informed.

The rules define "informed consent" as requiring the lawyer to communicate "adequate information and explanation about the material risks of and reasonably available alternatives." *See* Model Rule of Professional Conduct 1.0(e). But how does a lawyer *actually* do this?

There are two key questions. First, precisely what information must the lawyer provide? This will vary based on the facts and circumstances of the conflict. Typically, the lawyer must disclose the following: (a) the facts and circumstances giving rise to the situation; (b) an explanation of the material advantages and disadvantages of the lawyer's representation of both parties; and (c) the available options and alternatives. *See* Model Rule of Professional Conduct 1.0(e).

Second, what constitutes "reasonably adequate" communication? This answer too will vary with the facts and circumstances, specifically whether the client is: (a) experienced in legal matters; (b) experienced in making these types of decisions; and (c) independently represented by other counsel in giving the consent. *See* Model Rule of Professional Conduct 1.0 Comment 6.

You may be asking: what makes advance waivers of conflicts of interest different? Advance waivers, also called prospective waivers, are provisions in engagement letters whereby clients consent to and waive *future* conflicts of interest; *i.e.*, conflicts of interest that have not yet arisen.

Advance waivers have become more common, primarily for business reasons. In today's globalized world, law firms want to ensure that representing one client will not prohibit them from representing certain clients in the future. These firms want to ensure that the representation will not be the basis for a motion to disqualify if a conflict arises in the future.

Remember, though, consent to conflicts must be informed. With advance waivers, the conflict has not yet arisen, meaning the facts and circumstances of the conflict are not yet known. If there is no knowledge about the nature of the conflict, how can the consent be informed?

The key question is whether the client, at the time of signing the waiver, understood the material risks involved in consenting presently to the future, unknown conflict.

This requires the lawyer who seeks an advance waiver to explain to the client the types of future representations that *might* arise, as well as the possible adverse consequences of such future representation. The lawyer should include as much detail as possible about the specific types of conflicts that may arise. In addition, the explanation should include what measures the lawyer will take to keep from harming the client if the conflict does arise. The more detailed and comprehensive, the more likely the waiver will be valid.

This case study will allow you to explore what constitutes informed consent in obtaining advance waivers, the consequences of failing to get informed consent, and the best practices for using prospective waivers of conflicts of interest. You will also explore the policy reasons for and against advance waivers. You will have the opportunity to practice the following lawyering literacy skills: factual investigation, research, legal reasoning, legal problem solving, oral and written communication, client counseling, and policymaking and legal reform.

As with each case study in this book, the more effort you put into the role you are assigned, the more you will gain in substantive knowledge and practical experience. To get the most out of this case study, work through each part in the order presented, and do not read ahead.

THE CASE STUDY

You are a junior, non-equity partner at a large, Chicago law firm. One Sunday afternoon, you see in your email a request to check for conflicts; it looks like this:

From: Conflicts Check <conflictscheck@lawfirm.com>
Date: Sat, Dec 30, 2017 at 5:37PM
Subject: New Conflicts Check
To: All Lawyers & Staff <allemployees@lawfirm.com>

New Client Name: Manufacturing Company

Other Names/DBA: Manufacturing Company, LLC

Subsidiaries: N/A

Parent Company: N/A

Principles: Mrs. Sally CEO; Mr. Charlie CFO; Board Members X, Y, Z

Opposing Party/ies Name: Municipality

New Names/DBA: City of Municipality

Subsidiaries: N/A

Parent Company: N/A

Principles: N/A

Matter: Manufacturing Company wishes to retain Law Firm to represent it in a qui tam action, to which Municipality is an intervenor.

Originating Partner: Jane Partner, California office

You recall that you have done employment law work for Municipality (one of the plaintiffs) on and off for several years, including the review of several compensation agreements a few months ago. You quickly review the file and note that, at the start of your work, Municipality signed a prospective conflicts of interest waiver as part of the firm's standard engagement letter. You decide that the conflict in this new matter is therefore not an issue but that you will confirm your decision with your firm's in-house ethics counsel the next day.

On Monday morning, you raise the issue with ethics counsel, who agrees that because of the prospective waiver, the firm's representation of the defendant in the new matter is okay. You hear nothing more about the case until six months later, when ethics counsel calls early one morning and asks if you currently are doing work for Municipality. You tell ethics counsel that yes, you are involved in representing Municipality as a defendant in a Title VII action brought by several emergency responders.

Ethics counsel is livid and tells you that Municipality may seek to disqualify your firm from representing Manufacturing Company in the *qui tam* action based on your simultaneous representation of Municipality in the Title VII action.

PART ONE: IS THE ADVANCE WAIVER VALID?

1. Your day is not off to a good start; you are scheduled to make equity partner very soon, and now you worry your standing at the firm is at risk. You decide to review the advance waiver from Municipality's engagement letter. It provides:

> Conflicts with Other Clients. Law Firm has many attorneys and multiple offices. We may *currently or in the future represent one or more other clients (including current, former, and future clients) in matters involving* Municipality. We undertake this engagement on the condition that we may represent another client in a matter in which *we do not represent* Municipality, even if the interests of the other client are adverse to Municipality (including appearance on behalf of another client adverse to Municipality in litigation or arbitration) and can also, if necessary, examine or cross-examine Municipality personnel on behalf of that other client in such proceedings or in other proceedings to which Municipality is not a party *provided* the other matter is not substantially related to our representation of Municipality and in the course of representing Municipality we have not obtained confidential information of Municipality material to representation of the other client. *By consenting to this arrangement, Municipality is waiving our obligation of loyalty to it so long as we maintain confidentiality and adhere to the foregoing limitations.* We seek this consent to allow our Firm to meet the needs of existing and future clients, to

remain available to those other clients and to render legal services with vigor and competence. Also, if an attorney does not continue an engagement or must withdraw therefrom, the client may incur delay, prejudice or additional cost such as acquainting new counsel with the matter.

The waiver seems comprehensive and reasonable to you. It excludes substantially related matters and instances where the firm has obtained confidential information that is material to the representation giving rise to any future conflict. The waiver also seems to be written unambiguously in plain language. You wonder why ethics counsel is worried. Might the waiver be invalid? Consider the arguments on both sides of this question, and be prepared to advocate for both sides in class. Use the hints below only if you have difficulties after searching on your own.

> **HINT:** Review Comment 22 to Illinois Rules of Professional Conduct Rule 1.7 (remember, you are in the Chicago office). Can you find it from this page?
>
> http://www.illinoiscourts.gov/legal.asp

> **YOUR HOMETOWN:** Are there lawyers in your family or circle of friends? Send them an email, explaining that you are studying advance waivers of conflicts, and ask if they use such waivers in the usual course of their practice. Ask why or why not. See if they are willing to share the language they use. Compare your responses with those of your classmates, taking into consideration the practice area, size of firm, geography, and other factors. Do certain practice areas and firm sizes use these waivers more often? Is the use of these prospective waivers limited to multi-office big firms in big cities with business clients? Can you think of why smaller firms might use advance waivers?

2. After reviewing and thinking about Comment 22 to Illinois' Rule 1.7, you have some doubts about the validity of the waiver Municipality signed. Specifically, you wonder what would ever constitute informed consent for purposes of prospective waivers to conflicts. How could any client's consent to something that has not yet happened ever be "informed," as the rules require? Make a list of the facts and circumstances you believe must be present to constitute informed consent to an advance waiver. Can these requirements ever be satisfied before the conflict arises? (If not, you don't believe advance waivers will ever be valid!)

> **HINT:** In recent years, practitioners and scholars alike have considered what facts and circumstances should be present to find that advance waivers are valid. *See* https://www.americanbar.org/content/dam/aba/events/professional_responsibility/2015/May/Conference/Materials/clearly_enforceable_future_conflicts_waivers_bloomberg_bna.authcheckdam.pdf

> **YOUR HOMETOWN:** Research whether the ethics rules in your jurisdiction expressly permit advance waivers. Does your jurisdiction have an ethics opinion issued by the regulatory bar or a case covering advance waivers of conflicts of interest? What does it require for the waiver to be valid? Would Municipality's waiver likely be upheld in your jurisdiction?

3.   The changing nature of the way business is done throughout our world is one of the reasons for the rise of advance waivers to conflicts of interest. Clients and law firms are larger and more global; legal practices are more specialized; and the cost of legal services has increased. Based on these, and other factors, consider and be prepared to discuss the pros and cons of advance waivers *for both* clients and law firms. What do you believe is the best policy, overall, for the use of advance conflicts waivers to best serve our legal system?

PART TWO: IF NOT, WHAT ARE THE CONSEQUENCES?

Now you really are worried. What are the consequences for your firm (and you) if the advance waiver Municipality signed is not valid? (Think carefully about what this means; your firm is involved in two representations that give rise to a conflict of interest, for which you do not have consent.) Consider these questions.

1.   Does it matter that you and the lawyer representing Manufacturing Company against Municipality are in different offices?

> **HINT:** Review Illinois Rules of Professional Conduct Rule 1.10.
>
> http://www.illinoiscourts.gov/legal.asp

2.   Can you get consent now? Whose consent would you need? Is it realistic to think this is a possibility?

> **HINT:** Review Comments 14 and 15 to Illinois Rules of Professional Conduct Rule 1.7.
>
> http://www.illinoiscourts.gov/legal.asp

3. You talk to the partner representing Manufacturing Company against your client about getting consent now. However, before you can decide whether to seek consent, Municipality files a motion to disqualify your firm from representing Manufacturing Company in the *qui tam* action. If your firm is disqualified, what are the consequences? Reputational? Financial? Are there other consequences?

> **HINT:** Review the Restatement (Third) of the Law Governing Lawyers § 37 (2000).

4. What is the likely outcome of Municipality's motion to disqualify your firm in the *qui tam* action? Draft a summary, as if you were writing for the court, on the issue of whether the advance waiver constitutes informed consent. (You need not write a full opinion; focus on the narrow issue of whether waiver is valid based on the facts and circumstances presented.)

> **HINT:** Review the intermediate, appellate court opinion in *Sheppard, Mullin, Richter & Hampton, LLP v. J-M Manufacturing Co.*, 198 Cal.Rptr.3d 253 (2016) at Appendix A. (Your summary may or may not come to the same conclusion as the *Sheppard Mullin* court.)

5. The best lawyers are those who fully understand and appreciate the other side's argument. Write a summary, again as if you were writing on behalf of the appellate court, taking the opposite side from that which you took above.

> **HINT:** Re-review the intermediate, appellate court opinion in *Sheppard, Mullin, Richter & Hampton, LLP v. J-M Manufacturing Co.*, 198 Cal.Rptr.3d 253 (2016) at Appendix A.

PART THREE: HOW TO AVOID DISQUALIFICATION IN THE FUTURE

1. To avoid future such issues, and the potential loss of millions of dollars in legal fees, your firm is considering a prohibition on all advance waivers of conflicts. You wonder whether this extreme step is a good business practice, or even necessary. What recommendations would you make, based on your experience in this case, to increase the probability that such a waiver will be upheld?

2. Did your recommendations include counseling clients prior to signing advance waivers? What specifically would you say to a client who is about to sign an advance waiver? Be prepared to role play in class, both as lawyer and client.

3. Several months later, you receive a call from a disgruntled employee of a large manufacturing company that just opened a plant nearby. The employee wants to bring a wrongful termination action against the company. You believe this is a winning case for your firm and perhaps could support a large class action. Although you typically represent employers, you want to take the case. However, you do not want to preclude your firm from doing other work for the company in the future. Draft an advance conflicts waiver for the employee that will help facilitate such future representation.

> **HINT:** The New York City Bar has an excellent opinion on point that may help you in drafting your waiver.
>
> https://www2.nycbar.org/Publications/reports/show_html_new.php ?rid=442
>
> (At the time of this publication, Illinois had no such opinion.)

DOCUMENTS USED IN THE CASE STUDY

Appendix A: *Sheppard, Mullin, Richter & Hampton, LLP v. J-M Manufacturing Co.*, 198 Cal.Rptr.3d 253 (2016) (edited)

APPENDIX A

SHEPPARD, MULLIN, RICHTER & HAMPTON, LLP v. J-M MANUFACTURING CO., 198 CAL.RPTR.3D 253 (2016)

**Sheppard, Mullin, Richter & Hampton, LLP
v. J-M Manufacturing Co.**

198 Cal.Rptr.3d 253 (2016)

COLLINS, J.

INTRODUCTION

Appellant J-M Manufacturing Company, Inc. (J-M) appeals from a judgment in favor of its former attorneys, Sheppard, Mullin, Richter & Hampton, LLP (Sheppard Mullin). Sheppard Mullin sought recovery of attorney fees relating to litigation in which Sheppard Mullin represented J-M. Sheppard Mullin was disqualified from that litigation because, without obtaining informed consent from either client, Sheppard Mullin represented J-M, the defendant in the litigation, while simultaneously representing an adverse party in that case, South Tahoe Public Utility District (South Tahoe), in unrelated matters. * * * J-M argued that as a result of Sheppard Mullin's violation, J-M did not owe Sheppard Mullin outstanding attorney fees and Sheppard Mullin should return to J-M all attorney fees paid pursuant to the agreement.

The trial court ordered the case to arbitration based on the parties' written engagement agreement. A panel of three arbitrators. . .denied J-M's request for disgorgement of fees paid, and ordered J-M to pay Sheppard Mullin's outstanding fees. The trial court confirmed the award and J-M appealed. . . .,

* * *

BACKGROUND

A.   The underlying litigation: the Qui Tam Action

In 2006, a qui tam action was initiated against J-M and Formosa Plastics Corporation U.S.A. on behalf of approximately 200 real parties in interest. . . .

* * *

Sheppard Mullin represented J-M in the Qui Tam Action for sixteen months, litigating motions, conducting discovery, reviewing documents, and conducting an extensive internal investigation at J-M. It billed J-M nearly $3.8 million for approximately 10,000 hours of work.

B. Conflict waiver provision

[B]efore J-M retained Sheppard Mullin, (Sheppard Mullin lawyers) Daly and Kreindler ran a conflicts check to determine whether Sheppard Mullin had represented any of the real parties in interest identified in the Qui Tam Action. They discovered that Jeffrey Dinkin, a Sheppard Mullin labor-and-employment partner, had done work for South Tahoe, one of the municipal intervenors in the Qui Tam Action. * * * South Tahoe signed an engagement agreement with Sheppard Mullin in 2002, and it renewed that agreement in 2006. The agreement had a broad advance conflict waiver provision similar to the one in the J-M agreement, discussed below. Dinkin did occasional, as-needed labor and employment work for South Tahoe between 2006 and November 2009.

When Sheppard Mullin's conflict check for J-M revealed that South Tahoe was a client, Daly and Kreindler consulted with an assistant general counsel to Sheppard Mullin. That unidentified attorney informed them that South Tahoe had "agreed to an advance conflict waiver and that Sheppard Mullin had done no work for [South Tahoe] for the previous five months (since November 2009)." In addition, Daly and Kreindler discussed the issue with Ronald Ryland, Sheppard Mullin's general counsel, "who analyzed [South Tahoe's] conflict waiver and informed us that it allowed us to represent J-M in the Qui Tam Action."

Daly met with [South Tahoe representative] Eng for two hours on March 4, 2010, to discuss a draft engagement agreement. The draft contained the advance conflict waiver provision that ultimately was included in the final engagement agreement. It stated, "*Conflicts with Other Clients*. Sheppard, Mullin, Richter & Hampton LLP has many attorneys and multiple offices. We may *currently or in the future represent one or more other clients (including current, former, and future clients) in matters involving [J-M]*. We undertake this engagement on the condition that we may represent another client in a matter in which *we do not represent* [J-M], even if the interests of the other client are adverse to [J-M] (including appearance on behalf of another client adverse to [J-M] in litigation or arbitration) and can also, if necessary, examine or cross-examine [J-M] personnel on behalf of that other client in such proceedings or in other proceedings to which [J-M] is not a party *provided* the other matter is not substantially related to our representation of [J-M] and in the course of representing [J-M] we have not obtained confidential information of [J-M] material to representation of the other client. *By consenting to this arrangement, [J-M] is waiving our obligation of loyalty to it so long as we maintain confidentiality and adhere to the foregoing limitations*. We seek this consent to allow our Firm to meet the needs of existing and future clients, to remain available to those other clients and to render legal services with vigor and competence. Also, if an attorney does not continue an engagement or must withdraw therefrom, the client may incur delay, prejudice or additional cost such as acquainting

new counsel with the matter." (Italics added except for word "provided.")
We refer to this as the "conflict waiver provision."

According to Daly, Eng carefully reviewed the entire draft agreement with
him, and she "did not ask me any questions or express any concern about
the advance conflict waiver." Eng declared that Sheppard Mullin attorneys
never discussed the conflict waiver provision with her, nor did they explain
it. Eng also said the Sheppard Mullin attorneys assured her there were no
conflicts in representing J-M in the Qui Tam Action. J-M's practice was to
ensure that its outside attorneys had neither potential nor actual conflicts
of interest. Although Eng made a number of handwritten edits related to
the fee provisions, and also edited the paragraph preceding the conflict
waiver provision, she did not edit the conflict waiver provision. She
ultimately executed the engagement agreement (the Agreement) on March
8, 2010, and sent it to Daly by email.

C. South Tahoe raises the conflict of interest in the Qui Tam Action

Dinkin began actively working for South Tahoe again on March 29, 2010.
Between March 2010 and May 2011, Sheppard Mullin billed South Tahoe
for 12 hours of work, including telephone conversations and work on
employment matters.

In March 2011, Day Pitney, counsel for South Tahoe in the Qui Tam Action,
wrote a letter to Sheppard Mullin asserting that Sheppard Mullin had a
conflict as a result of its simultaneous representation of J-M and South
Tahoe. In response to the Day Pitney letter, Sheppard Mullin took the
position that South Tahoe had agreed to an advance conflict waiver in its
engagement agreement with Sheppard Mullin and therefore no conflict
existed. Day Pitney's position was that there was an actual conflict. In
April 2011, Day Pitney informed Sheppard Mullin that South Tahoe
planned to bring a motion to disqualify Sheppard Mullin from the Qui Tam
Action.

* * *

D. Sheppard Mullin is disqualified as counsel in the Qui Tam Action

South Tahoe's disqualification motion in the Qui Tam Action was heard on
June 6, 2011. The district court tentatively ruled that the advance waiver
in South Tahoe's engagement agreement with Sheppard Mullin was
invalid. In its tentative ruling, the court cited Rule 3–310(C)(3), which bars
an attorney from representing clients in adverse positions without the
informed written consent of each client. The court referred to the
engagement agreement letters between Sheppard Mullin and South Tahoe,
and said that "the prospective waivers contained within the 2002 and 2006
letters were ineffective to indicate South Tahoe's informed consent to the
conflict at issue here." The court added, "The Court cannot conclude that
South Tahoe was in any way close to 'fully informed'" about the conflict
with J-M.

* * *

On July 14, 2011, the district court granted South Tahoe's motion to disqualify Sheppard Mullin.

E.   The present action

After Sheppard Mullin was disqualified, J-M took the position that J-M was not required to pay Sheppard Mullin any fees that were outstanding at the time of the disqualification. J-M also demanded that Sheppard Mullin return all fees relating to the Qui Tam Action that J-M had already paid.

In June 2012, Sheppard Mullin filed an action against J-M. . . [seeking] approximately $1.3 million as payment for services rendered to J-M in the Qui Tam Action and related matters. . . J-M . . .sought disgorgement of fees previously paid to Sheppard Mullin. [The parties went to arbitration, per the engagement letter. A panel of three arbitrators assumed that Sheppard Mullen's failure to get a waiver from J-M at the time the South Tahoe conflict arose was an ethical violation, but found that "Sheppard Mullin's conduct was not so serious or egregious as to make disgorgement or forfeiture of fees appropriate." J-M appealed.]

* * *

DISCUSSION

* * *

C.   Sheppard Mullin violated Rule 3–310

* * *

Rule 3–310(C)(3) provides that an attorney "shall not, *without the informed written consent of each client* . . . [r]epresent a client in a matter and at the same time in a separate matter accept as a client a person or entity whose interest in the first matter is adverse to the client in the first matter." (Italics added.) " 'Informed written consent' means the client's . . . written agreement to the representation following written disclosure." (Rule 3–310(A)(2).)

* * *

[T]he essential facts are not in dispute. Sheppard Mullin partner Jeffery Dinkin did work for South Tahoe before the parties entered into the Agreement. Sheppard Mullin's conflicts check revealed Dinkin's work for South Tahoe before Sheppard Mullin gave the Agreement to J-M, but Sheppard Mullin concluded that there was no reason to disclose this relationship to J-M. J-M signed the Agreement without knowing that Sheppard Mullin represented South Tahoe in unrelated matters. The parties disagree about whether South Tahoe was a "former" client or a "current" client at the time the Agreement was signed. However, it is undisputed that three weeks after J-M signed the Agreement, Dinkin began working for South Tahoe again, so there is no question that there was an actual conflict at that point. Sheppard Mullin was disqualified from the Qui Tam Action as a result.

Sheppard Mullin argues that it proceeded as required by Rule 3–310(C)(3): "The conflict waiver in the Engagement Agreement waives both current *and* future conflicts. Waivers of current and future conflicts are commonplace and enforced by California and other courts." The conflict waiver provision in the Agreement stated that Sheppard Mullin "may currently or in the future represent one or more other clients (including current, former, and future clients) in matters involving [J-M]." The Agreement allowed Sheppard Mullin to engage in conflicting representations "*provided* the other matter is not substantially related to our representation of [J-M] and in the course of representing [J-M] we have not obtained confidential information of [J-M] material to representation of the other client." It continued, "By consenting to this arrangement, [J-M] is waiving our obligation of loyalty to it so long as we maintain confidentiality and adhere to the foregoing limitations."

What Sheppard Mullin ignores, however, is that Rule 3–310(C)(3) requires *informed* written consent. "Where. . . a fully informed consent is not obtained, the duty of loyalty to different clients renders it impossible for an attorney, consistent with ethics and the fidelity owed to clients, to advise one client as to a disputed claim against the other."

Here, the undisputed facts demonstrate that Sheppard Mullin did not disclose *any* information to J-M about a conflict with South Tahoe. The Agreement includes a boilerplate waiver that included no information about any specific potential or actual conflicts. Dinkin was working for South Tahoe while Sheppard Mullin was defending J-M against South Tahoe in the Qui Tam Action. It strains credulity to suggest that the Agreement constituted "*informed* written consent" of actual conflicts to J-M, when in fact Sheppard Mullin was silent about any conflict.

Even assuming Sheppard Mullin was not representing South Tahoe at the time it entered into the agreement with J-M, Sheppard Mullin nonetheless began performing additional work for South Tahoe three weeks later. It did not inform either client of this actual conflict. Because "waiver must be informed, a second waiver may be required if the original waiver insufficiently disclosed the nature of a subsequent conflict."* * *

[S]heppard Mullin cites *Visa U.S.A., Inc. v. First Data Corp.*, (N.D. Cal. 2003) 241 F.Supp.2d 1100, [which]. . .involved a motion to disqualify [the law firm] Heller in a case involving a potential future conflict. First Data, which was developing a system to processes credit card transactions, asked Heller to represent it in a patent infringement action pending in Delaware. The parties recognized a possible future conflict with Visa, with whom Heller had a longstanding relationship. Heller informed First Data that although it saw no current conflict in representing First Data in the Delaware action, it would only agree to represent First Data if First Data agreed to permit Heller to represent Visa in any future disputes, including litigation, that might arise between First Data and Visa. First Data agreed, and signed an engagement letter that clearly stated these terms.

About a year later, Visa sued First Data in California for trademark infringement and other claims. First Data moved to disqualify Heller as counsel for Visa in the California case, arguing that Heller's violation of Rule 3–310(C) required automatic disqualification.

The district court observed that an advance waiver of potential future conflicts, such as the one executed by First Data and Heller, is permitted under California law, even if the waiver does not specifically state the exact nature of the future conflict. [T]he *Visa* court emphasized that the "only inquiry that need be made is whether the waiver was fully informed," and noted that "[a] second waiver by First Data in a non-related litigation would only be required if the waiver letter insufficiently disclosed the nature of the conflict that subsequently arose between Visa and First Data."

[T]he *Visa* court identified factors to be taken into account in evaluating whether full disclosure was made and the client made an informed waiver, such as the breadth of the waiver, the temporal scope of the waiver, the quality of the conflicts discussion between the attorney and the client, and the nature of the actual conflict. Applying these factors, the *Visa* court found that the waiver was sufficient because Heller had identified the adverse client and disclosed as fully as possible the nature of any potential conflict. Heller had also explained that in the event of an actual conflict, it would represent Visa in any matters against First Data, including litigation. The court found that First Data signed the waiver with fully informed consent to any conflict with Visa.

[V]isa stand[s] in sharp contrast to the facts here. Unlike Heller in . . .*Visa,* Sheppard Mullin did not disclose the circumstances regarding a potential or actual conflict with South Tahoe to either J-M or South Tahoe. The Sheppard Mullin attorneys on the Qui Tam Action were aware the firm had a relationship with South Tahoe, and even sought advice from firm counsel as to whether it had to be disclosed before J-M signed the Agreement. The conflict waiver provision in the Agreement did not mention South Tahoe. Instead, it broadly waived all current and future conflicts with any client: "*Conflicts with Other Clients.* Sheppard, Mullin Richter & Hampton LLP has many attorneys and multiple offices. We may currently or in the future represent one or more other clients (including current, former, and future clients) in matters involving [J-M]. . . . By consenting to this arrangement, [J-M] is waiving our obligation of loyalty to it so long as we maintain confidentiality and adhere to the foregoing limitations."

The facts here therefore are not analogous to . . .*Visa,* because Sheppard Mullin (1) failed to inform J-M about any potential or actual conflict with South Tahoe, and (2) did not obtain J-M's informed, written consent to continued representation despite the actual conflict that occurred while Sheppard Mullin was working for J-M and South Tahoe at the same time. Written consent to all potential and actual conflicts in the absence of any

PART ONE: ARE THERE RULES ON POINT?

1.   You recall from your Professional Responsibility course in law school
     that there are general rules governing what a lawyer can say publicly
     about a trial; find the relevant rule in West Virginia. Summarize the
     rule's prohibitions on trial publicity that apply to all lawyers, including
     prosecutors. Also summarize what is expressly permitted. Create a
     hypothetical fact scenario and provide examples, based on your fact
     pattern, of what public statements about the case would be permitted
     and what would be prohibited. Use the hints below only if you have
     difficulty after searching on your own.

> **HINT:** Review West Virginia Rules of Professional Conduct Rule
> 3.6 and the comments.
>
> http://www.courtswv.gov/legal-community/court-rules/professional-
> conduct/contents.html

> **YOUR HOMETOWN:** Research the analogous rule in the
> jurisdiction in which you intend to practice (or in your hometown).
> Are the guidelines for trial publicity the same as those under the
> West Virginia Rules of Professional Conduct?

2.   You also know that Rule 3.8 speaks to trial publicity and extrajudicial
     statements by a prosecutor. Summarize the rule's prohibitions on trial
     publicity that apply specifically to prosecutors. Using your
     hypothetical fact scenario from above, or a new one, provide a few
     examples of statements that would be permitted and prohibited.

     Also, explain any duties prosecutors have with respect to others
     involved in the prosecution to prevent them from making
     inappropriate public statements.

> **HINT:** Review West Virginia Rules of Professional Conduct Rule
> 3.8(f) and the comments.
>
> http://www.courtswv.gov/legal-community/court-rules/professional-
> conduct/contents.html

> **YOUR HOMETOWN:** Research the analogous rule in the
> jurisdiction in which you intend to practice (or in your hometown).
> Are the guidelines for extrajudicial statements by prosecutors the
> same as those under the West Virginia Rules of Professional
> Conduct?

Part Two: The Duke Lacrosse Case

1. You decide to research the Duke Lacrosse case to better understand what concerns your boss has about media statements. Using Google or other search engine of your choice, find a national media source summarizing the case. What is your sense of the case based on this article? Do you find the piece credible? If you compare several of the articles you find, do you get the same perspective? Do the facts change?

> **HINT:** You likely will find many articles from your search. How do you evaluate information you find online? If you are unfamiliar with evaluating such research, review this resource from The University of Akron School of Law:
>
> http://law.uakron.libguides.com/evaluating_websites

2. You learn from your research that the prosecutor in the Duke Lacrosse case, Mike Nifong, was disbarred by the North Carolina State Bar for his actions in the case. You want more specifics, from original source material. You believe the official order issuing the discipline is the best place to find out exactly what Prosecutor Nifong did that led to his discipline. Find this order.

> **HINT:** The North Carolina State Bar, the regulatory body that licenses lawyers in North Carolina, maintains a searchable database of orders of discipline from 1999 to the present. Can you find this database from the State Bar's homepage?
>
> https://www.ncbar.gov/
>
> Once you find the search page, search by "Nifong":
>
> https://www.ncbar.gov/lawyer-discipline/search-past-orders/orders-in-discipline-and-disability-cases/

3. You locate the Order of Discipline, which is called "Amended Findings of Fact, Conclusions of Law and Order of Discipline." You are surprised to find that it is 24 pages long. Begin by reviewing the Order and summarizing the facts. Take careful notes and be prepared to explain the facts, in layman's terms, in class.

> **HINT:** Were you able to locate the Order? If not, try this link:
>
> https://www.ncbar.gov/handlers/DisciplinaryOrderHandler.ashx?url=\06DHC35.pdf

4. Now that you better understand the facts of the Duke Lacrosse incident and the actions leading to the disciplinary action, focus on the public statements Prosecutor Nifong made. Reread the Order and take

careful notes of Prosecutor Nifong's violations of North Carolina Rules 3.6 and 3.8(f). Consider the specific statements made by Prosecutor Nifong, and consider whether you agree that the statements violated the prohibitions on pre-trial publicity. Do certain statements seem more egregious than others?

PART THREE: A MEDIA POLICY FOR YOUR OFFICE

1. Having reviewed the Nifong Order of Discipline and considered the extrajudicial statements that were problematic for Prosecutor Nifong, do you agree with your boss that your office should have a media policy? What should be included? Draft a policy to present to your boss. Be prepared to exchange your policy with your classmates for comment and review.

> **HINT:** The National District Attorney's Association publishes standards titled "National Prosecution Standards," which may be helpful in considering what to include in your media policy:
>
> http://www.ndaa.org/pdf/NDAA%20NPS%203rd%20Ed.%20w%20 Revised%20Commentary.pdf

> **YOUR HOMETOWN**: Does the local prosecutor's office in your hometown or law school's jurisdiction have a media policy? Contact them and find out. Explain that you are doing research for your Professional Responsibility course. (You may even be able to obtain a contact name for the office from your professor or your law school's career services office.) Ask for a copy of the policy if one exists.

PART FOUR: ELECTING PROSECUTORS

1. You observed in the Nifong Order of Discipline that the Hearing Committee noted, early in the Findings of Fact, that "Nifong was engaged in a highly-contested political campaign to retain his office." (Line 4, https://www.ncbar.gov/handlers/DisciplinaryOrderHandler. ashx?url=\06DHC35.pdf)

    The United States is the only country where voters elect prosecutors.[1] The theory behind electing prosecutors, in short, is that elections create "a promising environment for real accountability to the voters."[2] Today, there are over 2,400 elected prosecutors in the county.[3] What are your thoughts on electing prosecutors? What are the

---

[1] Michael J. Ellis, *The Origins of the Elected Prosecutor*, 121 YALE L.J. 1528, 1530 (2012).

[2] Ronald F. Wright, *Beyond Prosecutor Elections*, 67 SMU L. REV. 593, 599 (2014).

[3] *See* http://wholeads.us/justice/, a project by the Reflective Democracy Campaign on Who Prosecutes America (last visited March 7, 2018).

pros and cons of prosecutorial elections? Consider that 95% of elected prosecutors are white and only 1% are women of color.[4]

> **YOUR HOMETOWN:** Are state prosecutors elected in your home jurisdiction (or the jurisdiction in which you intend to practice)? How about the jurisdiction where your law school if located?

> **LEARN MORE:** You may be interested to know that David Freeman, Prosecutor Nifong's lawyer in the North Carolina State Bar hearing, has stated publicly that he does not believe Nifong was influenced to act based on the upcoming election.[5] There are many scholarly articles and other resources regarding whether prosecutors should be elected; some you may wish to review include:
>
> Amita Kelly, *Does It Matter That 95 Percent of Elected Prosecutors Are White*, NAT'L PUBLIC RADIO, July 18, 2015, *available at:*
>
> https://www.npr.org/sections/itsallpolitics/2015/07/08/420913118/does-it-matter-that-95-of-elected-prosecutors-are-white
>
> Ronald F. Wright, *Beyond Prosecutor Ethics*, 67 SMU L. REV. 593 (2014), *available at:*
>
> http://scholar.smu.edu/cgi/viewcontent.cgi?article=1044&context=smulr
>
> Jeffrey Toobin, *The Milwaukee Experiment*, THE NEW YORKER, May 11, 2015, *available at:*
>
> https://www.newyorker.com/magazine/2015/05/11/the-milwaukee-experiment

---

[4] *Id.*

[5] North Carolina Advocates for Justice Presentation at Wake Forest University School of Law, November 9, 2017.

CHAPTER 6

THE FACEBOOKING JUDGE

<table>
<tr><td>ISSUE AREAS:
Judicial Discipline Process, Judicial Elections, Judicial Speech, Public Education About Courts and the Judicial System, Social Media Use by Lawyers and Judges</td></tr>
</table>

LEARNING OBJECTIVES:

1. Analyze social media use by judges under the relevant professional ethics rules.

2. Assess the importance of public awareness about courts and the judicial system.

3. Describe the judicial discipline process and analyze disciplinary orders.

4. Draft professional ethics rules and policies for social media use by judges.

5. Evaluate rules governing judicial campaign speech and judicial speech about pending cases.

6. Explain the process for reforming judicial ethics rules.

7. Identify concerns associated with an elected judiciary.

8. Locate online judicial discipline records and opinions.

BACKGROUND

This case study exposes you to the ways lawyers and judges use social media. The study also will help you understand when this activity might subject a lawyer or judge to professional discipline. While most jurisdictions have not yet adopted rules specifically governing social media, disciplinary bodies have applied general rules, sometimes with unexpected (and unpleasant) outcomes for lawyers and judges.

Keep in mind as you work through this exercise that popular social media tools such as Facebook, Instagram, and Twitter *did not exist* when most professional conduct rules governing lawyer and judicial ethics were drafted and adopted. For example, Facebook was founded in 2004, Instagram in 2010, and Twitter in 2006. By comparison, the American Bar Association Model Rules of Professional Conduct were adopted by the ABA House of Delegates in 1983, two decades before Facebook made its debut. In addition, the ABA Model Code of Judicial Conduct was adopted in 1990. Although both the Rules and the Code have been amended occasionally over the years, certainly neither was originally drafted with social media usage in mind.

Social media may be a relatively new phenomenon, but it has quickly become a leading source for the public to obtain information about news and government. According to a 2016 study conducted by the Pew Research Center, a majority of American adults received their news via social media sources. Indeed, social media has become such a powerful mechanism for influencing public opinions that companies like Facebook and Twitter were brought before the Senate Judiciary Committee in late 2017 to testify about Russian influence on the 2016 presidential election via the media platforms. And, of course, many elected officials use social media to communicate directly with the public, perhaps most famously President Trump.

Lawyers and judges increasingly are using these tools to communicate about legal services and to educate the public. Most law firms and courthouses have public social media accounts. Many individual lawyers have online profiles through professional networking sites such as LinkedIn, in addition to Facebook pages or Twitter feeds, for advertising and obtaining new clients, and even for personal use. The use of social media by individual judges is seen mostly in states with elected judiciaries, where many judges have official campaign Facebook pages and/or Twitter feeds. (More than half of the United States elects at least a portion of their judiciary.)

In some ways, social media can be seen as a tool that democratizes who can afford to run for judicial office, since it is free (*e.g.* Facebook or Twitter) or low-cost (*e.g.* LinkedIn) and widely adopted by the public. The use of social media also raises the prominence of judges. For example, Texas Supreme Court Justice Don Willett was named the Tweeter Laureate by the state legislature in 2015, and he was regularly featured in popular media for his Twitter use until he silenced his account after being nominated to the United States Court of Appeals for the Fifth Circuit in late 2017. (He had posted nearly 26,000 tweets to 130,000 followers at the time.) However, judges and lawyers alike have found themselves subject to discipline for social media use. Thus, it is important to be aware of potential pitfalls when engaging in this sort of communication.

This case study will allow you to contemplate some of these pitfalls and provide you with an opportunity to practice the following lawyering literacy skills: analyzing legal documents, drafting policies and professional conduct rules, legal problem solving, policymaking and legal reform, reflective practice research, statutory/rule analysis, and oral and written communication.

As with each case study in this book, the more effort you put into the role you are assigned, the more you will gain in substantive knowledge and practical experience. Work through each part of this case study in the order presented, and do not read ahead in order to get the most out of the exercise.

THE CASE STUDY

You are a lawyer at a mid-sized Texas law firm where you specialize in defending lawyers and judges accused of misconduct. One afternoon, Judge Michelle Slaughter, 405th District Court in Galveston, Texas, calls your office and asks for her help. She explains that as part of her judicial campaign (judges are selected via partisan elections in Texas), she promised to keep citizens updated about court cases through her official Facebook page. She regularly posts publicly-available information about proceedings in her courtroom and finds that voters appreciate learning about what happens. You follow her Facebook page, and have seen posts like these from time to time:

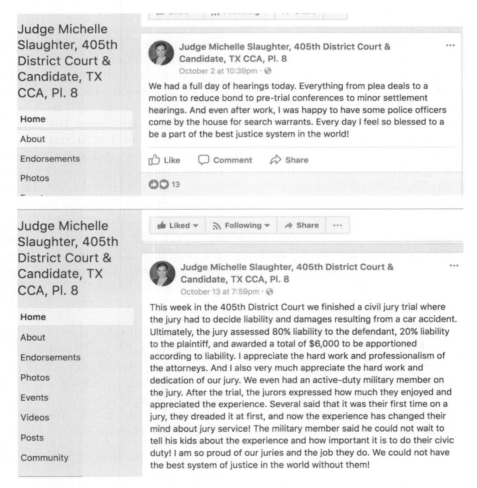

Judge Slaughter explains that recently she was disciplined by the Texas State Commission on Judicial Conduct after she posted information about a pending case. The Commission found that she violated two Canons of the Texas Code of Judicial Conduct. She was publicly admonished and ordered to engage in judicial education about the use of social media.

Judge Slaughter believes that she did not violate the Canons, and that the sanction compromises government transparency as well as violates her First Amendment rights. She also feels that the sanction will shut down an important and cost-effective method for educating the public about courthouse proceedings, which she believes is essential in states like Texas with an elected judiciary. She wants to know if there is anything she can do to challenge the Commission's determination.

You agree to look into the matter, and you ask her to send any relevant documents. She emails you a copy of the Commission's Public Admonition and Order of Additional Education (Appendix A of this case study). Review the document carefully, and then begin working through the steps below.

PART ONE: THE JUDICIAL DISCIPLINE SYSTEM

1. Every state and the District of Columbia has a separate judicial discipline system, most based upon the ABA Model Code of Judicial Conduct. In Texas, the Commission on Judicial Conduct is charged with administering judicial discipline. Sanctions can include private or public reprimands, education, supervision/mentoring, monetary fines, and even removal from office. You have reviewed the Public Admonition and Order of Additional Education in Judge Slaughter's case. Is she able to challenge the sanctions? If so, what procedural steps must be taken? What can you learn from online research about the Texas State Commission on Judicial Conduct? How do complaints come to the Commission? Use the hints below only if you get stuck.

> **HINT:** Start by searching for the Texas State Commission on Judicial Conduct website. Here is a link if you cannot find it by searching: http://www.scjc.texas.gov/ What information is available? Who is the primary audience for this website?

> **HINT:** Much of the information contained on the Commission website is intended for the public, and to help individuals file complaints about judges. Click on Frequently Asked Questions to look for information on how judges can appeal a decision: http://www.scjc.texas.gov/faqs/ Make a note of the process to file an appeal, including any deadlines and required pleadings. Also note the format of the appeal hearing, including the procedural rules followed.

> **YOUR HOMETOWN:** See if you can find a website for the official body handling judicial discipline in the state of your hometown (or, if your hometown is in Texas, look up a state where you may practice law, that you recently visited, or that otherwise interests you). What is the disciplinary body called in that jurisdiction? Is it also a Commission, or is it something different? Does it follow a

similar process for handling complaints, and for appealing discipline sanctions? If not, how does it differ from Texas? Why might states follow different procedures?

LEARN MORE: The National Center for State Courts maintains a clearinghouse for information about judicial ethics and discipline. You can learn more about the judicial discipline process in all fifty states plus the District of Columbia here:

http://www.ncsc.org/cje

PART TWO: JUDICIAL CONDUCT CODES AND ADVISORY OPINIONS

1. You now know the procedure for handling Judge Slaughter's appeal. You must also determine the key facts and relevant legal standards to argue on appeal. She has been disciplined for her postings on Facebook. The Commission lists two Canons of the Texas Code of Judicial Conduct. You want to review a complete listing of all Canons of the Texas Code of Judicial Conduct. Can you locate it? Is the Code available on the Commission's website?

    HINT: The highest court of each state adopts the judicial code of conduct. Begin by looking at the website for the Texas Supreme Court. Try finding the Texas Code of Judicial Conduct there. If you need help, go to

    http://www.txcourts.gov/rules-forms/rules-standards/

2. Download the Texas Code of Judicial Conduct, and review the Canons. When was the Code adopted? Did Facebook exist at the time the Code was adopted? Do any of the Canons specifically address social media use?

3. In addition to codes of conduct, most jurisdictions maintain databases of advisory opinions on questions of judicial ethics. See if you can locate advisory opinions for Texas judicial ethics issues.

    HINT: In addition to maintaining the Code of Judicial Conduct, the Texas Supreme Court also publishes ethics advisory opinions here:

    http://www.txcourts.gov/publications-training/judicial-ethics-bench-books/judicial-ethics-opinions/

    Review the general index; do any of these opinions appear to offer guidance about the use of social media by judges?

> **LEARN MORE:** All federal judges are governed by the Code of Conduct for United States Judges, *available at* http://www. uscourts.gov/judges-judgeships/code-conduct-united-states-judges, except for the Supreme Court, which is not bound by any official code of conduct. Why do you think the Supreme Court is the only judicial body not bound by this sort of code? Should the Court adopt a code of conduct?

> **YOUR HOMETOWN:** Search to locate the code of judicial conduct and advisory ethics opinions for the same state you used to learn about the discipline process in Part One. Compare it with the Texas Canons. How is it similar? How is it different? Would a judge be subject to discipline for social media posts under this code?

4.　Have you found any specific guidance from the Texas Code of Judicial Conduct or advisory opinions about social media use by judges? Where else might you look for guidance?

> **HINT:** The National Center for State Courts offers many resources for state court judiciaries:
>
> http://www.ncsc.org/Topics/Media/Social-Media-and-the-Courts/ Social-Media/Home.aspx

PART THREE: JUDICIAL ELECTIONS

1.　Federal judges are appointed, but more than half the states elect at least a portion if not all of their judiciary. Some states, including Texas, hold partisan elections, and campaigns can be costly, ranging from tens of thousands to hundreds of thousands of dollars. (The 2015 Pennsylvania Supreme Court election saw nearly $16 million in campaign spending.) What concerns might we have about judges who must solicit campaign contributions in order to hold office? Should states with judicial elections permit judges greater access to tools like social media, which reach the public for far less expense than traditional television and radio advertising or mailings and flyers?

> **LEARN MORE:** Retired US Supreme Court Justice Sandra Day O'Connor, as well as retired Texas Supreme Court Chief Justice Wallace B. Jefferson, both have offered harsh critiques of the judicial election system, and proposed reforms.
>
> Justice O'Connor's proposal for judicial selection is set forth here:
>
> http://iaals.du.edu/quality-judges/projects/oconnor-judicial-selection-plan

> You can read a lengthy interview with Chief Justice Jefferson here:
>
> https://www.theatlantic.com/national/archive/2013/10/a-broken-system-texass-former-chief-justice-condemns-judicial-elections/280654/

PART FOUR: THE APPEAL

1. Based upon the research you conducted for Part One, you now know that Judge Slaughter has 30 days from the date the Commission issued its disciplinary order to appeal by filing a written request with the Chief Justice of the Supreme Court of Texas for the appointment of three appellate justices to act as a Special Court of Review. The Special Court of Review will hold a de novo trial, which means that the case will be heard anew, as if the Commission had never acted.

    Prepare an opening statement for the trial. To do so, begin by listing the key arguments you will make on appeal, and the arguments that the Commission is likely to advance. For purposes of this case study, you do not need to conduct additional research. Assume that this case presents issues of first impression, *i.e.*, no court has ever issued an opinion about how Canons 4A and 3B(10) of the Texas Code of Judicial Conduct should be applied in the context of social media. Be prepared to deliver a five-minute opening statement at your next class. Your professor may assign some students to represent Judge Slaughter and some to represent the Commission.

PART FIVE: REFORM

1. Your work on this case leads you to believe that courts should consider adopting uniform policies to help guide judges when they want to communicate with the public via platforms like Facebook or Twitter. Draft a two to three paragraph policy with best practices for judicial use of social media, including guidance for communicating with the public about court proceedings. As you draft, consider that new platforms may be developed in the future, so write with this in mind.

2. You also believe judges would benefit from a specific professional conduct rule to govern social media use. A safe harbor rule would protect judges who want to use social media as a public education or campaigning tool from facing the stress and expense of defending discipline charges that ultimately are overturned, as was the case for Judge Slaughter. Draft a revision to the ABA Model Code of Judicial Conduct or to the Texas Code of Judicial Conduct based upon the policy you prepared. How will you go about proposing a new rule? Describe the process for getting the rule adopted.

HINT: There are two possible paths for reform to judicial conduct rules.

First, you might submit your proposal to the American Bar Association, which promulgates the Model Code of Judicial Conduct. To learn more about this process, review this article, which briefly describes the process when the ABA revisited the Code of Judicial Conduct in 2003 and ultimately revised the Code in 2007:

https://www.americanbar.org/content/dam/aba/migrated/judicial ethics/resources/JudicialWinterArticle.authcheckdam.pdf

Even if the ABA adopted your proposal, however, you would still need to convince the highest court in the relevant jurisdiction to also adopt the rule. As you can see from this chart showing state-by-state adoption of the 2007 revisions, this can be a lengthy process:

https://www.americanbar.org/groups/professional_responsibility/ resources/judicial_ethics_regulation/map.html

Second, you might approach the highest court in the state directly with your proposal, or request an advisory opinion. For example, in Texas, the Texas Center for Legal Ethics maintains opinions on ethics issues:

https://www.legalethicstexas.com/Ethics-Resources/Opinions.aspx

The Texas Commission on Professional Ethics issues opinions pursuant to Texas Government Code § 81.091 which provides that "[t]he committee shall, either on its own initiative or when requested to do so by a member of the state bar, express its opinion on the propriety of professional conduct other than on a question pending before a court of this state."

LEARN MORE: Judges are not alone in facing potential discipline for use of social media. Lawyers have been disciplined in a range of circumstances, including violation of advertising rules, client confidentiality obligations, and improper contact with judges. The New York State Bar Association released a comprehensive guide for lawyers, Social Media Guidelines, in 2017:

http://www.nysba.org/socialmediaguidelines17/

DOCUMENTS USED IN THE CASE STUDY

Appendix A: Texas State Commission on Judicial Conduct, Public Admonition and Order of Additional Education

APPENDIX A

TEXAS STATE COMMISSION ON JUDICIAL CONDUCT, PUBLIC ADMONITION AND ORDER OF ADDITIONAL EDUCATION

BEFORE THE
STATE COMMISSION ON JUDICIAL CONDUCT

CJC No. 14-0820-DI & 14-0838-DI

PUBLIC ADMONITION
AND
ORDER OF ADDITIONAL EDUCATION

HONORABLE MICHELLE SLAUGHTER
405TH JUDICIAL DISTRICT COURT
GALVESTON, GALVESTON COUNTY, TEXAS

During its meeting on April 8-9, 2015, the State Commission on Judicial Conduct concluded a review of the allegations against the Honorable Michelle Slaughter, Judge of the 405th District Court, Galveston, Galveston County, Texas. Judge Slaughter was advised by letter of the Commission's concerns and provided a written response. Judge Slaughter appeared with counsel before the Commission on April 9, 2015, and gave testimony. After considering the evidence before it, the Commission entered the following Findings and Conclusion:

FINDINGS OF FACT

1. At all times relevant hereto, the Honorable Michelle Slaughter was Judge of the 405th Judicial District Court in Galveston, Galveston County, Texas.

2. At all times relevant hereto, Judge Slaughter maintained a public Facebook page which displayed a photograph of the judge wearing her judicial robe; featured a photograph of the Galveston County Courthouse; described the judge as a "public figure" and as "Judge, 405th Judicial

District Court;" and identified the judge as "Judge Michelle M. Slaughter" on each comment the judge posted.[1]

3.   According to Judge Slaughter, the Facebook page was set up with the intent that it would be "the most efficient way to fulfill [her] campaign promise and [her] own goals of educating the public about our courts."

4.   Judge Slaughter's Facebook page was publicly accessible to any person who wished to view it online.

The *Wieseckel* Case

5.   From April 28-30, 2014, the criminal jury trial of *State v. David M. Wieseckel* was held in Judge Slaughter's court.

6.   David Wieseckel was charged with unlawful restraint of a child for allegedly keeping a 9-year-old boy in a 6 foot by 8 foot wooden enclosure, which had been used as the child's bedroom.

7.   On April 26, 2014, Judge Slaughter posted the following comment on her Facebook page:

> "We have a big criminal trial starting Monday! Jury selection Monday and opening statements Tues. morning."

8.   The following day, in response to the post described above, a person named Jeff Bodie posted the following comment on Judge Slaughter's Facebook page:

> "One of my favorite Clint Eastwood movies is 'Hang 'Em High', jus [sic] sayin [sic] your honor....."[2]

9.   In a pre-trial hearing on April 28, 2014, the defendant's attorney argued a motion *in limine* to limit the use of the term "box" to describe the wooden enclosure at trial, contending that the term was prejudicial to the defendant and misstated the evidence.

10.   Judge Slaughter denied defense counsel's motion, stating the following:

> "Calling it a wooden enclosure – certainly the press has referred to it as 'The Boy in the Box' case, that sort of thing. So I don't think that there's going to be prejudice. The jury can make up their own minds as to what they believe that is."

11.   On April 28, 2014, after the jury had been selected, Judge Slaughter provided the jurors with oral instructions regarding their use of social media, including Facebook, and their access to any news stories about the case. The judge expressly admonished the jurors as follows:

> "During the trial of the case, as I mentioned before, you cannot talk to anyone. So make sure that you don't talk to anyone. Again, this is by any means of communication. So no texting, e-mailing, talking person to person or on the phone or Facebook. Any of that is absolutely forbidden."

---

[1] According to Judge Slaughter, she took down the "Judge Michelle M. Slaughter" Facebook page after receiving notice of the Commission's inquiry, which was sent on or about September 22, 2014. The Commission confirmed that the Facebook page appears to no longer be available online.

[2] Judge Slaughter informed the Commission that she was "shocked" to see Bodie's post and removed it as soon as she became aware of it through the defendant's motion to recuse; however the post remained on the site at least through September 10, 2014.

12. In addition the judge provided written instructions to the jury that included the following admonition:

> "Do not make any investigation about the facts of this case. ... All evidence must be presented in open court so that each side may question the witnesses and make proper objection. This avoids a trial based upon secret evidence. *These rules apply to jurors the same as they apply to the parties and to me* (the judge)." (emphasis added).

13. On April 28, 2014, Wieseckel elected to have Judge Slaughter determine his punishment in the event of his conviction.

14. On April 29, 2014, after the first day of testimony, Judge Slaughter posted the following comments on her Facebook page:

- "Opening statements this morning at 9:30 am in the trial called by the press 'the boy in the box' case."

- "After we finished Day 1 of the case called the 'Boy in the Box' case, trustees from the jail came in and assembled the actual 6"x8' 'box' inside the courtroom!"

- "This is the case currently in the 405th!" [this post included a link to a *Reuters* article entitled: "Texas father on trial for putting son in a box as punishment."]

15. At time of Judge Slaughter's April 29, 2014 Facebook post, the "'actual' box" referenced in her comments had not yet been admitted as an exhibit or as evidence at trial.[3]

16. Furthermore, the *Reuters* article that was linked to the judge's Facebook post contained extraneous offense[4] information, which the judge had instructed the jury panel to disregard during jury selection, and which had not been admitted into evidence at trial at the time of the post.

17. On April 30, 2014, defense counsel filed a motion to recuse Judge Slaughter from the case, as well as a motion for mistrial, claiming that Judge Slaughter had improperly commented about the *Wieseckel* trial on her Facebook page and had improperly posted a link to a *Reuters* article covering the trial.

18. Judge Slaughter was removed from the *Wieseckel* case that same day after a visiting judge assigned to hear defense counsel's recusal motion granted it.

19. Following Judge Slaughter's recusal, the *Wieseckel* case was transferred to another court and the judge in that court granted the defendant's motion for mistrial.

20. Judge Slaughter's Facebook posts regarding the *Wieseckel* case, as well as her recusal and the subsequent mistrial, received widespread media attention critical of her conduct.

---

[3] The following day, during an in-chambers hearing with prosecutors and the judge, defense counsel objected to the admission of the "box" as a demonstrative exhibit, arguing that the evidence was repetitive. Judge Slaughter overruled the objection and later admitted the "box" into evidence.

[4] Under Rule 404b of the Texas Rules of Evidence, "Evidence of other crimes, wrongs or acts is not admissible to prove the character of a person in order to show action in conformity therewith. It may, however, be admissible for other purposes, such as proof of motive, opportunity, intent, preparation, plan, knowledge, identity, or absence of mistake or accident, provided that upon timely request by the accused in a criminal case, reasonable notice is given in advance of trial of intent to introduce in the State's case-in-chief such evidence other than that arising in the same transaction." Extraneous offenses include other crimes the accused may have been arrested and/or convicted of.

21. Judge Slaughter defended her public Facebook comments about the *Wieseckel* case, arguing to the Commission that the purpose of her comments was to promote "transparency" and to "encourage individuals to come watch the proceedings."

22. In addition, Judge Slaughter asserted that her Facebook comments did not suggest her probable decision in the *Wieseckel* case because her comments were true and based on publicly available information.

23. The judge further explained that she selected her words carefully to make it clear that it was the media who referred to the case as the "boy in the box" case, not her.

24. Judge Slaughter added that in her opinion, the *Reuters* article was "written in a very objective way – just the facts – and not slanted in any way towards either side," and that her public comments did not serve as a basis for any suggestion of any probable decision she would make in the case.

Other Facebook Posts

25. On February 5, 2014, Judge Slaughter posted the following comment on her Facebook page regarding a matter pending in her court:

    > "We have a jury deliberating on punishment for two counts of possession of child pornography. It is probably one of the most difficult types of cases for jurors (and the judge and anyone else) to sit through because of the evidence they have to see. Bless the jury for their service and especially bless the poor child victims."

26. Judge Slaughter defended this Facebook post by explaining that the jury had already heard all the evidence on punishment and was deliberating in the case.

27. Judge Slaughter further asserted that the post "merely point[ed] out an obvious fact that sitting through any child pornography case is difficult."

28. On May 13, 2014, following her recusal from the *Wieseckel* case, Judge Slaughter posted the following comment on her Facebook page:

    > "We finished up sentencing today with a very challenging defendant."

29. Judge Slaughter defended this post by arguing that "[u]sing the phrase 'very challenging' does not give rise to any indication that [she] treated [the defendant] unfairly;" and that the post "referred to a case that was no longer pending or impending" in her court and, as such, "there was nothing to suggest [her] probable decision in that case."

RELEVANT STANDARDS

1. Canon 3B(10) of the Texas Code of Judicial Conduct states, in pertinent part: "A judge shall abstain from public comment about a pending or impending proceeding which may come before the judge's court in a manner which suggests to a reasonable person the judge's probable decision on any particular case…This section does not prohibit judges from making public statements in the course of their official duties or from explaining for public information the procedures of the court."

2. Canon 4A the Texas Code of Judicial Conduct states: "A judge shall conduct all of the judge's extrajudicial activities so that they do not: (1) cast reasonable doubt on the judge's capacity to act impartially as a judge; or (2) interfere with the proper performance of judicial duties."

3. Article V, §1-a(6)A of the Texas Constitution provides that a judge may be disciplined for "willful or persistent violation of rules promulgated by the Supreme Court of Texas, incompetence in performing the duties of the office, willful violation of the Code of Judicial Conduct, or willful or persistent conduct that is clearly inconsistent with the proper performance of his duties or casts public discredit upon the judiciary or administration of justice."

CONCLUSION

The Commission concludes from the facts and evidence presented that Judge Slaughter's decision to post comments and a link to a media story on her Facebook page regarding the *Wieseckel* case and other matters pending before her court was inconsistent with the proper performance of her duties as a judge. Judges have a duty to decide every case fairly and impartially. Judicial independence, impartiality and integrity must be seen in order for the public to have confidence in the legal system. Despite her contention that the information she provided was public information, Judge Slaughter cast reasonable doubt upon her own impartiality and violated her own admonition to jurors by turning to social media to publicly discuss cases pending in her court, giving rise to a legitimate concern that she would not be fair or impartial in the *Wieseckel* case or in other high-profile cases. The comments went beyond providing an explanation of the procedures of the court and highlighted evidence that had yet to be introduced at trial. Judge Slaughter's Facebook activities interfered with her judicial duties in that, as a direct result of her conduct, a motion to recuse was filed and granted requiring the judge to be removed from the *Wieseckel* case. The judge's recusal then led to the granting of a motion for mistrial so that the case could be retried in its entirety before another judge. Judge Slaughter's conduct in the case was clearly inconsistent with the proper performance of her duties and cast public discredit upon the judiciary or administration of justice in light of the considerable negative media attention given the case and her posting. The Commission therefore concludes that Judge Slaughter's conduct constituted a willful and persistent violations of Canons 3B(10) and 4A of the Texas Code of Judicial Conduct, and Article V, Section 1-a(6) of the Texas Constitution.

****

In condemnation of the conduct described above that violated Canons 3B(10) and 4A of the Texas Code of Judicial Conduct and Article V, §1-a(6)A of the Texas Constitution, it is the Commission's decision to issue a **PUBLIC ADMONITION AND ORDER OF ADDITIONAL EDUCATION** to the Honorable Michelle Slaughter, Judge of the 405th District Court, Galveston, Galveston County, Texas.

Pursuant to this Order, Judge Slaughter must obtain **four (4) hours** of instruction with a mentor, in addition to her required judicial education. In particular, the Commission desires that Judge Slaughter receive this additional education in the area of the proper and ethical use of social media by judges.

Judge Slaughter shall complete the additional **four (4) hours** of instruction received above within **sixty (60) days** from the date of written notification of the assignment of a mentor. It is Judge Slaughter's responsibility to contact the assigned mentor and schedule the additional education.

Upon the completion of the **four (4) hours** of instruction described herein, Judge Slaughter shall sign and return the Respondent Judge Survey indicating compliance with this Order. Failure to complete, or report the completion of, the required additional education in a timely manner may result in further Commission action.

5

Pursuant to the authority contained in Article V, §1-a(8) of the Texas Constitution, it is ordered that the actions described above be made the subject of a **PUBLIC ADMONITION AND ORDER OF ADDITIONAL EDUCATION** by the Commission.

The Commission has taken this action in a continuing effort to protect public confidence in the judicial system and to assist the state's judiciary in its efforts to embody the principles and values set forth in the Texas Constitution and the Texas Code of Judicial Conduct.

Issued this 20th day of April, 2015.

ORIGINAL SIGNED BY

_____

Honorable Steven L. Seider, Chair
State Commission on Judicial Conduct

6

CHAPTER 7

SUBSTANCE ABUSE AND LAWYER DISCIPLINE

ISSUE AREAS:

Duty to Report Misconduct, Lawyer Assistance Programs, Lawyer Disciplinary System, Self-Regulation, Substance Abuse, Work-Life Balance

LEARNING OBJECTIVES:

1. Analyze the ethical duty to report certain lawyer misconduct.

2. Develop and refine advocacy skills.

3. Draft relevant documents for a lawyer disciplinary hearing.

4. Evaluate the ethics and efficacy of the duty to report and self-regulation.

5. Identify resources available to lawyers with substance abuse and mental health concerns.

6. Recognize the impact of substance abuse, mental health, and work-life balance issues within the legal profession.

7. Understand and evaluate the lawyer discipline process.

BACKGROUND

This case study will prepare you handling attorney misconduct cases, and help you better respond to pressures associated with the practice of law, including substance abuse issues and work-life balance.

It may come as somewhat shocking news to learn that the profession you have chosen is among the highest for mental health issues and substance abuse. A 2016 study conducted by the Hazelden Betty Ford Foundation in partnership with the American Bar Association found that over 36% of licensed, practicing lawyers consume alcohol at levels that correlate with "hazardous drinking or possible alcohol abuse or dependence" (compared with just over 10% among other professions). The same study revealed high levels of depression (45.7%) and anxiety (61.1%) among lawyers. The full results of the study, published in the *Journal of Addiction Medicine*, can be found here: http://journals.lww.com/journal addictionmedicine/Fulltext/2016/02000/The_Prevalence_of_Substance_Use_and_Other_Mental.8.aspx.

It may, perhaps, be more shocking to learn that even if you follow all of the ethics rules, you can be disciplined as a lawyer for failing to report problematic behavior of *other* lawyers. Many states follow American Bar Association Model Rule 8.3, which requires a lawyer to report behavior that "raises a substantial question as to that lawyer's honesty, trustworthiness or fitness as a lawyer in other respects. . . ." One famous case from the late 1980s involved an Illinois attorney, James Himmel. He was suspended from practice for a year by the Illinois Supreme Court because he did not report financial misconduct by another lawyer. (The other lawyer refused to turn over $35,000 from a settlement to his client.) Why do you think this reporting requirement exists?

As a practicing lawyer, if you observe another lawyer whose ability to competently represent clients seems compromised because of substance abuse, or mental health issues, what should you do? If the jurisdiction where you practice has adopted Model Rule 8.3, you may be obligated to report the lawyer to the jurisdiction's lawyer discipline authority. Is there anything short of discipline that might be done? What if you struggle with these issues personally? (Given the results of the recent study discussed above, you may very well face these issues in your own life and inevitably will know lawyers who do. You may even know those who do now.) One option is to seek help from a local lawyers assistance program, typically run by a state bar association or under a mandate from a state supreme court. You will learn more about these support programs through this case study.

This case study exposes you to the lawyer discipline process while providing you an opportunity consider the implications of substance abuse for lawyers. You will practice several lawyering literacy skills: analyzing legal documents, drafting legal pleadings, factual investigation, legal problem solving, reflective practice research, statutory/rule analysis, and oral and written communication, including advocacy and argumentation.

THE CASE STUDY

You are bar counsel for the Florida Bar, where you handle complaints against lawyers that may constitute violations of the Rules Regulating the Florida Bar. In this role, you work with staff investigators to determine whether a violation has occurred. If you find sufficient evidence, you forward the complaint to one of the Bar's grievance committees, which will conduct additional investigation. The Florida Bar has more than 80 local circuit grievance committees. The grievance committees include lawyers and lay people appointed by the Board of Governors of the Florida Bar, usually comprised of nine members. The grievance committee reviews evidence and may hear from witnesses, including the lawyer under investigation, and then takes one of several courses of action:

(1) dismiss the complaint;

(2) find no probable cause with a letter of advice to the lawyer;

(3) recommend mediation/arbitration if a fee is in dispute;

(4) issue an admonishment for minor misconduct;

(5) recommend diversion to a practice and professionalism program such as ethics school or rehabilitative treatment;

(6) recommend staying the proceeding until resolution of a parallel criminal or civil proceeding; or

(7) find probable cause, which means the case will be tried.

You arrive at work one morning and find a newspaper article from the Florida Sun Sentinel on your desk. The first sentence of the article reads: "A 33-year-old man who told deputies he was a 'DUI Defense Lawyer' was charged with driving drunk with a 3-year-old child in his SUV." The full article is available here: http://articles.sun-sentinel.com/2013-08-22/news/ fl-palm-dui-with-kid-20130822_1_deputy-palm-beach-county-sheriff-driver. You look up Attorney Hauserman and see that he has no discipline record and that he is a member in good standing of the Florida Bar.

PART ONE: BAR COMPLAINT

1. What steps, if any, should you now take after reviewing the newspaper article? Has any violation of the Rules Regulating the Florida Bar occurred? Where can you locate the rules? Use the hints below only if you have difficulties after searching on your own.

> **HINT:** You can search the full set of Rules Regulating the Florida Bar here: https://www.floridabar.org/rules/rrtfb/ Do any Rules apply to this situation? Identify the Rules and make note of them.

2. After reviewing the Rules, you determine you need more information before you can assess whether a violation has occurred. What additional information would be helpful to you? Describe briefly how you will go about conducting your investigation.

> **YOUR HOMETOWN:** What rules would apply in your hometown?

> **LEARN MORE:** Most jurisdictions have a mandatory reporting requirement for lawyer behavior that "raises a substantial question as to that lawyer's honesty, trustworthiness or fitness as a lawyer in other respects." *See* ABA Model Rule 8.3(a). A lawyer who knows of this behavior by another lawyer must report it, typically to the relevant bar authority. This means it is not enough to simply report the behavior to a supervisor within a law practice or legal organization. Note that this reporting obligation is placed upon all attorneys, not just those working for a state bar association. That said, when this information is learned during the course of a

> lawyer's participation in "an approved lawyers assistance program" it is protected, and reporting is not required. *See* ABA Model Rule 8.3(c).

3. Assume you decide to wait until the drunk driving charges are processed. A few months later you learn that Attorney Hauserman pled guilty to the charge of Driving Under the Influence, with a sentence of nine months house arrest, one year of probation, community service, and DUI school.

    You decide that it is now appropriate to bring this matter before the Grievance Committee. Draft the Complaint. Refer to Exhibit A as a model.

PART TWO: ROLE PLAY—BAR GRIEVANCE COMMITTEE HEARING

1. The Grievance Committee has reviewed the Complaint and decides to set the matter for a hearing. Your professor will assign you one of three roles to conduct a mock Grievance Committee hearing during class: (1) lawyer for Mr. Hauserman; (2) lawyer for the Florida State Bar; or (3) hearing judge.

    Lawyers should draft a 1–2 page motion arguing that the Grievance Committee decide the case in their client's favor. Lawyers should be prepared to present a 10-minute opening statement, followed by a 5-minute closing statement. Hearing judges will prepare a 1–2 page opinion explaining their decision in the matter. Lawyers and hearing judges should address legal arguments and recommended discipline, if any. You do not need to conduct additional research for this exercise.

PART THREE: APPEAL

1. Assume that the Grievance Committee found probable cause and set the matter for trial. The next step would be to draft a formal complaint and file it with the Florida Supreme Court. The Court will appoint a circuit or county judge to oversee the case. This judge will make a report, with recommendations, to be approved by the Florida Supreme Court. The report is filed with the Supreme Court and it is reviewed by the Board of Governors. The Board and the respondent each have 60 days to appeal the report's decision.

    In the real case, Attorney Hauserman entered into a plea agreement. See if you can find a copy of the plea agreement. (By the way, it is ok if you want to consider the information in the plea agreement as you prepare your assignment in Parts One and Two, but you do need not be confined by it if you find other arguments to support your client's case or if you have different recommendations for discipline.) Was the plea agreement ultimately approved by the Florida Supreme Court? Use the hint below only if you get stuck.

> **HINT:** The Florida Bar maintains extensive discipline records for all attorneys. You can find the discipline record for Attorney Hauserman here:
>
> https://www.floridabar.org/directories/find-mbr/profile/?num=41137

PART FOUR: LAWYERS ASSISTANCE PROGRAMS

1. If a lawyer struggles with substance abuse, mental health, or wellness issues, what resources are available for support? Explore the resources available to Florida attorneys, and describe how an attorney might use these resources to avoid a situation like that of Attorney Hauserman.

> **HINT:** Each state has a lawyers assistance program. The American Bar Association maintains a list of the programs and other resources here:
>
> https://www.americanbar.org/groups/lawyer_assistance/resources/lap_programs_by_state.html

> **YOUR HOMETOWN:** What resources are offered by the state bar where your hometown is located?

> **LEARN MORE:** Reflect upon issues related to substance abuse among the legal profession, which is significantly higher than other professions, as well as the ethics and efficacy of a discipline system made up entirely of members of the regulated profession. Why do you think this is the case? Read more in this New York Times article published in 2017, *The Lawyer, the Addict* by Eilene Zimmerman, available here:
>
> https://www.nytimes.com/2017/07/15/business/lawyers-addiction-mental-health.html

DOCUMENTS USED IN THE CASE STUDY

Appendix A: Florida Bar Complaint